MIRACLE IN THE MIRROR

MIRACLE IN THE MIRROR

Mark Buntain

with

Ron Hembree
and Doug Brendel

79

BETHANY HOUSE PUBLISHERS
Minneapolis, Minnesota 55438
A Division of Bethany Fellowship, Inc.

Scripture quotations are taken from the King James
Version of the Bible.

Calcutta Mission of Mercy

Mark Buntain
with Ron Hembree and Doug Brendel

Library of Congress Catalog Card Number 81-70999

ISBN 0-87123-352-5

Published by Bethany House Publishers
6820 Auto Club Road, Minneapolis, Minnesota 55438

Printed in the United States of America

Contents
MIRACLE IN THE MIRROR

To RANEE N. EDWARDS,
NITA'S MOTHER
*Her indomitable and fervent
faith helped make Nita's
miracle possible.*

Prologue

Our tiny walk-up apartment, perched three floors over the suffering city of Calcutta, was silent. The helpers had long since returned to their homes in the sultry tropical night. Those we had taken into our own home to help and love, had all gone to bed.

But for me, sleep would not come. Nita was still not back. She was out at an area church, ministering again, sharing her testimony again, as she had so many times.

Ever since she arrived in Calcutta, I had felt an unusual stirring in my spirit. My mind could not settle down. It kept churning, turning over and over the stories I had heard about her—and me. What could it all mean? Was I really linked to this girl by some immense, imponderable destiny?

I paced, praying for Nita, unable to escape my thoughts of her. She was a lovely young Sri Lankan, who had come to work for a few months in our hospital before returning to school in America. I knew she had a remarkable past—an incredible healing that several people had told me about, although I had never heard her tell the story herself. Now, as I prayed in the soft darkness, I sensed, deep in my spirit, that Nita's healing was only a fraction of the larger picture—a picture that included my own future.

"Dear God," I prayed, wringing my hands, "how am I

related to this girl? Does she really need me somehow?
What are you trying to say to me through this person?"

It was late when Nita finally returned, but my heart was
still longing to know the elusive answers to my questions. I
asked her to tell me her story.

We sat in the little living room on either side of a single
lamp, and in those wee hours she began to relate a
fantastic tale. As she talked, we both wept and laughed
and praised the Lord. Hours later, with dawn already
threatening to bring in another day, Nita finished her
account. There was an awesome presence of God in the
room, and we knelt together before the Lord, weeping and
praying and rejoicing in Him.

My eyes were opened that night. I began to see that
larger picture, of how Nita's story could, and would,
affect my own life's work—and, indeed, the entire continent of Asia.

I knew immediately that her story had to be told. It
became an unexplainable passion with me. But, who
should do it? Who could I get to capture the poignancy
and power of this spiritual drama?

The burden of the telling would not leave me alone. I
agonized before God and then He whispered to my spirit a
name.

I contacted my dear friend Ron Hembree, pastor of
Kennedy Road Tabernacle in Brampton, Ontario, and a
veteran professional writer. He had written my own
story,[1] and agreed to help me with this one.

Some time later, after Nita had returned to finish her
education in California, I returned to Canada. Before
many days had gone by, the three of us, Ron, Nita, and
myself, sat together, and again I heard the nearly unbeliev-
able story. We were swept up in it for hours, riding the ebb
and flow of its grief and glory, its fury and fantasy.

As I listened again, I knew in my heart that Nita Edwards was God's vessel for touching the teeming population of the turbulent Asian continent. And my own life, my own ministry, would never be the same.

This is Nita's miraculous story.

1. Ron Hembree, *Mark*. (Plainfield, N.J.: Logos, 1979).

PART I

And it shall come to pass afterward,
that I will pour out my spirit upon all flesh;
and your sons and your daughters shall prophesy,
your old men shall dream dreams,
your young men shall see visions...
Joel 2:28

Magistrate Edwards, Nita's Father

Nita at eight months

Nita with her mother before the accident

1
Faces on a Wall

Sri Lanka lies like a jewel off the southern coast of India, a beautiful bauble of unmolested natural charms, lapped by the warm waters of the Indian Ocean, cradled in her arms like a precious multicolored opal.

She was once known as Ceylon, before the years of harsh political reality and modern world tensions. For centuries the island has been a bastion of Buddhism, a land where seventy percent of the populace worship Buddha and the rest take care not to offend him.

Only two persons out of every thousand are Christians.

In Colombo, the capital city on the southern coast of Sri Lanka, live most of the island nation's people. It is a city approaching the modern age with its share of skyscrapers and international flights and tourism and crime.

But it was here in Colombo, in the middle 1950s, long before the advent of this modern age, when Sri Lanka was still Ceylon, when the island was still draped in its Buddhist past, that a loving God reached down through the shroud to touch a singular young man—and through him a nation, a continent, a world.

In a tough section of town there was a tiny Bible school, where a few Christians gathered to learn what they could of God's Word. They called their school the Ceylon Bible Institute, but it was hardly that; actually it was little more than a collection of old desks and chairs and tiny rooms where students studied and prayed and ate and slept.

One of the students, a firebrand named Colton Wickramaratne, had come from a village far outside Colombo and had managed to make a name for himself almost as soon as he arrived. He was a go-getter, always anxious to do more for the Lord, excited about moving forward, and ruffling feathers here and there as he went. Colton brought other problems with him too. For one thing, he was always struggling financially, and, to top it all off, his English was bad. Finally the school's harried administrators put him on probation for six months and remanded him to the custody of a local missionary family.

It was here that Colton finally took time to listen to God. Captive in his room, he spent long days in prayer. There, the Holy Spirit settled in and began a maturing work in Colton's life, establishing within this diminutive dynamo the strength of character his life's work would require. Day by day, Colton determined to draw closer to the heart of God. Hour after hour, their relationship deepened, as the Bible student opened himself more and more to the Father.

One evening as Colton sat in the missionary's home, alone in prayer, he felt a shift in the air, an unusual movement of the Spirit. Something told him it was different, but he couldn't explain why. He opened his eyes—as if to see the presence of God—but everything appeared to be the same: the same skinny bed, the rickety dresser with a ragged throw rug in front of it and an old lamp on top of it . . . an ancient mirror hanging on the wall.

The wall.

Colton felt his eyes drawn to it.

It was no longer the dull blank wall it had been. Instead he saw an arrangement of unfamiliar faces looking back at him. Colton stared at the faces, astounded, silent. He did not recognize any of them. They were all obviously Westerners, white-faced men—except for one, a girl with dark lovely features, an Asian.

"These eight people," the Spirit of God said to him silently, "will touch Asia with the gospel. These eight people will be instrumental in a great Asian revival to come."

Colton watched, wide-eyed, as God continued to speak to his heart.

"You will meet each of these people," the inner voice continued. "But you are not to tell anyone what you have seen. . .until you meet the eighth and final person."

Colton squinted to remember every detail, but then the faces were gone as suddenly as they had appeared.

Deeply shaken, the young man fell to his knees and wept before the Lord, worshiping with a reverence he had never felt in his life. He knew he had been in the presence of the Almighty, and that the Almighty had deposited something so precious within him that even Colton could not yet estimate its value.

Colton Wickramaratne grew by bounds as a Bible student, taking on a small church and nurturing its growth. Over the next ten years he ascended to a place of leadership among the Full-Gospel pastors of Sri Lanka.

One by one, during a period of about ten years, the people he had seen in the vision began turning up, sometimes in unlikely places. He had never met any of the eight people before the vision, and now each new encounter filled Colton with awe. Still, he never said a word about the vision to any of them, for he had not yet met all eight.

It was after he met the seventh person that things changed. While the first seven people had appeared over the space of ten years, the eighth face did not. The young woman still did not present herself. Another ten years elapsed. Had God forgotten?

Colton's work went on, and his ministry progressed. He was now a recognized leader in the Asian religious world. But, he could not forget the face! He found himself looking for the eighth face in crowded churches, in airports, and on street corners. Still she did not appear.

Sometimes he wondered if he would recognize her at all; it had been so many years since the vision. Now, twenty years after the experience, he sometimes wondered if he would really ever be able to tell anyone about the experience.

And sometimes—in moments of weakness—he wondered if he had ever really seen the eighth face at all.

2
The Accident

It was a silly accident, really.

For an athlete like Nita to bump her way down the entire staircase on her rear end was—well, embarrassing. And yet everyone else in St. Bede's Hall, the entire dorm, heard the thump-thump-thump and the inevitable final crash, and of course they all came running out of their rooms at the head of the stairs to see what the commotion was about.

Nita had returned the day before from an inter-university athletic meet in India's Mandi Valley, high in the Himalayas, where she had led her team to every women's trophy but one. So it was ridiculous to fall in the first place, let alone to sit there at the foot of the stairs, and not be able to get up.

Her legs just wouldn't work and pain stabbed her spine until perspiration beaded her forehead.

In a few moments several housemates had scrambled to her aid and dragged her up to a standing position—she could tell she had hurt her leg or foot somehow, and badly—but with their help she began pulling, dragging herself back up the brass-plated stairway toward her room. She forced herself to laugh and chatter with her girlfriends, saying with a grimace that it had finally happened! (They say you can't live in St. Bede's Hall without taking a tumble down the grand staircase at least once.) Before she got to her room at least three or four of them had congratulated her again on the fabulous triumph at the meet the day before.

Behind the closed door of her room, still humiliated by the fall, Nita dumped herself in her desk chair and picked up a textbook. Final exams were only two weeks away, and she had to do well. She could just hear her mother telling her she had neglected her education in favor of the sports activities she loved, and Nita was determined to prove otherwise. After all, no one had forced her to come up to northern India from Sri Lanka for her schooling. She had wanted to travel, she still wanted to see the world, and she still wanted eventually to study psychology in a foreign land.

The pain pumped up from her big toe, through her leg and into her hip as she sat and studied, but the star athlete had been bruised dozens of times before in the combat of competitive sport, and had no time for fooling around with whatever this was. It didn't feel like torn ligaments or pulled muscles, so she didn't even peel off her white socks to take a look. This was really nothing compared to, say, how she felt after some of the hockey games her girls' team had played as practice skirmishes against men's teams. Men, the girls always said, will cheat when they fall behind, and Nita had taken her share of blows by the hockey stick. She was certainly used to a bruise now and then. It was all part of the thrill of competition, a thrill that she craved going into every game, and then savored coming out.

The entire school, beautiful and serene as it was, generated a certain electricity in Nita. The venerable old University of H.P. (Himachal Pradesh) was situated in a cluster of lush firs and cedars in the foothills of the Himalayas in temperate northern India—far from the staggering suffering of Asia. Nita, an Anglican by birth, was one of only three Protestants on campus—and the only Spirit-filled Christian at that—among eighteen Roman Catholics, twenty or so Tibetan Buddhists, and a mixture of Hindus, agnostics, and atheists from all over the world.

In what could have been an intimidating setting, Nita decided to live her faith with excitement and drink in every moment. She was known for her zany sense of fun and her inclination for good times. She was always included when big groups of students took off to go out for dinner. She had studied speech and drama, as well as foreign languages, at Trinity College in London before coming to India, and her outgoing nature, knowledge and agility made her one of the university's most popular young people.

Among Nita's favorites were the nuns and priests who conducted the campus chapel. She attended 6:15 mass every morning and sang proudly in the Catholic church choir from the stately choir loft—to the delight of the nuns. She learned the various prayers and rituals and sincerely made each service a time of true worship with Catholic friends.

She was fond of hiking up to Eagle Mount where the head priest lived, to spar with the little old man over theology, world affairs, and politics. He took to teasing her by calling her his "faithful Catholic," a preposterous nametag for a Spirit-filled Episcopalian from the Church of England. But he could sense her deep commitment to God, and he eventually served her holy communion in the

Catholic chapel—a strict taboo in Indian Catholicism.

Nita remained true to her Anglican heritage as well. Each Sunday morning she and her two Protestant friends made sandwiches and set out on foot to attend the nearest Episcopalian church some seven miles away. It was a huge old cathedral—empty and cold. The bishop's prepared sermons and somewhat pompous prayers echoed forlornly through the museum-like sanctuary each week. But even this weekly ritual somehow invigorated Nita. It was again part of the total experience, part of the adventure of life that she was inhaling so fully and deeply every day.

Still, from her first day on campus, Nita's personal testimony as a Christian was her foremost priority. She excused herself wherever tobacco or drugs or alcohol appeared on campus, avoiding the seamy parties that are part of every secular university in the world. She was known as a Christian with practical convictions; no one challenged that, because she would never compromise her faith.

Deep within her being, Nita also resolved to live an active positive Christianity, to spend herself in the service of the Lord, by giving help to the helpless wherever and whenever she could.

An entire mission field lay just beyond the campus, where Tibetan refugees were encamped in a government settlement. Having fled their own bloodthirsty government, when the Communists crushed their gentle land, these people now suffered the menaces of refugee life— disease, hunger, and depression. It was Nita's first encounter with true starvation. She often walked with friends to the hospital near the camp and ministered there, feeding the hungry bodies, and speaking words of hope, encouragement, and love in Jesus Christ to hungry hearts.

She became, true to form, a popular face in the refugee hospital. Eyes lit up in every ward she entered. She might stop to lift a lonely child to her bosom, or hold the hands of a tired old Tibetan man.

For Nita, these were the best of times.

Each day, her love affair with the entire university scene grew more impassioned—with every new tennis or cross-country victory, every hilarious storytelling session in the dorm, every exhilarating glide down the ski slopes. She was making life a blast at this formidable and fashionable old school—and both she and the school seemed to love it.

When Nita's giddy, victorious team returned to school the night before her accident, singing and shouting in the back of their huge open truck, staggering under the weight of their many trophies, and waking the entire campus, the jolly Irish principal had declared the next day a school holiday. Nita was vibrant as the heady celebration carried on, deep into a beautiful, fragrant moonlit night.

The team had slept late that morning then regrouped for a trip downtown, grateful for the unexpected holiday. They feasted on tandoori chicken and traditional Indian nan bread, and continued the exulting celebration of their victories. When finally the group decided to take in a movie, Nita headed back to campus, still brimming with delight. It was late afternoon.

As she bounded into the foyer at St. Bede's, she saw Bambi, a beautiful little two-year-old girl who was staying with the nuns for a while. Bambi's mother was going through a difficult time in her life so the child spent most of her time as an unofficial ward of the dormitory.

Bambi had become the doll baby of St. Bede's, a precious little visitor who was welcome at every bedroom door. She would stand at the bottom of the long, wide staircase and call toward the bedrooms on the upper level: "May I come up and play?" And someone invariably responded, "Yes, Bambi, come up and play in my room."

But this day there were no takers. Everyone was busy taking advantage of the holiday with studies or more pressing diversions. As Nita crossed the foyer toward the staircase, she saw Bambi's big brown eyes blink back the tears of disappointment and rejection, her lip pouting out just a little.

Nita's heart twitched. From the moment the child appeared at St. Bede's, Bambi had touched Nita in a special way. Every time she saw the child she thought of the little girl's father, gone now, unavailable to give his little Bambi the love she would need so desperately in the coming years. Nita knew the emptiness that could mean. She had lost her own father as well. . .and she could never quite get over the ache and the bitterness when she thought of how he died.

"Come on, let's go," Nita said to Bambi playfully as she got to the steps. "We'll go to my room."

Bambi smiled her fabulous tiny smile and grasped her friend's little finger. She knew that Nita kept toys and candy for her in the room, even if she did have to get busy and study.

Slowly they made their way up the stairs together, with Bambi's tiny fat legs stretching their best to make each new step. The two girls chatted excitedly all the way up, with Nita's eyes fastened on Bambi's plodding progress.

The top step somehow disappeared. Nita's legs slipped out from under her and tossed her face-down onto the upper few steps. In a split second she realized she had lost hold of the baby, and she rolled over on her back to reach for her. Bambi had fallen, and stayed put on a single step, her eyes wide open with surprise—but she was intact. Nita pushed herself with her elbows to stand up, but she never regained her footing. It all happened so suddenly, and she wound up on the floor, looking up at the beautiful architecture of the immense high ceiling in the foyer. Bambi was screaming, and the entire place was in an uproar.

Nita's vanity took the real blows. Here she was, the ranking female athlete, a model of coordination, who had just thudded down St. Bede's staircase on her behind!

Peeved and in pain she studied intently for the rest of the day in the seclusion of her room, ignoring the hurt in her legs and lower back. On a trip to the bathroom, just down the hall, she found she lost her equilibrium and fell down after every three or four steps—but her mind was fixed on her exams, and she returned to her books. Who had time for a checkup anyway?

But the creeping anguish had begun. By nightfall Nita was falling down with every step she took.

The next day she found a walking stick, and it was funny at first, how she manoeuvered herself around.

"Nita! What's this now?"

"Oh, haven't you heard? I've joined the stockbrokers in London!"

There was a bit of prestige, after all, in relying on a cane for a few days. But in her room, as she kept up her studies for final exams, the pain pounded with increasing intensity. Then a deadly numbness began to creep up her legs.

For the grueling schedule of exams, the walking stick was worthless. Nita arranged for friends to be on hand for each excursion. They helped her out of St. Bede's and into each classroom, then back again after the exam. Each moment was more excruciating than the last. Desperately Nita clung to her mental faculties, gripping her pencil and pressing out each paragraph. She was not about to let a stupid fall down St. Bede's stairs destroy a semester of work—and open the door for Mother to make more comments.

The pain and the numbness, however, were both advancing ominously like twin terrors. Before the finals ended, Nita could no longer sit upright to take her tests. The pain stabbed her so viciously that she had to lean over on one side, stretching herself sideways in her chair, to write the tests. After three hours in that position she could not pull herself up. She looked down at her legs. She could see them, but she could neither feel them nor make them move. Two friends dragged her out of the chair and carried her back to St. Bede's, up the stairs, and into her room.

One of Nita's friends, Sister Andrew, dropped by. She was grim.

"Nonsense, Andy," Nita chided her. "It's a sprain or something. I just need to stay off my feet for a while—after finals."

"This won't do," the young nun said tersely, as if she hadn't heard a word. "You're going to see a doctor."

A car was pulled up in minutes, and Sister Andrew assembled a group of girls to carry the beautiful, awkward cargo back down the hated stairs. With some trouble they eventually stuffed her in the car, and they headed for the best orthopedic specialist in northern India, a Jewish doctor who worked out of a big Seventh Day Adventist hospital. Nita sat awkwardly as the doctor examined her legs, squeezing and kneading each joint in careful succession—toe, ankle, knee, hip. There was no response.

"But doctor, I have pain," Nita insisted. "It's drawing up my leg from my big toe."

The doctor fell silent and looked evenly at Sister Andrew for a moment. Then he gently turned the patient over, laying her flat on her stomach. Beginning at the neck, he ran his finger lightly along the length of her spine. Before he could pull away, Nita had let out a horrible scream.

"I want X-rays!" the doctor barked shortly, pointing his nervous nurse out the door. "I want the proofs immediately. Don't wait for them to dry."

The X-ray machine had turned out four pictures, and the doctor held them dripping up to the light. There was no intricate study to be done. The pictures were quite clear. Two discs in the lower lumbar region of Nita's back had been completely crushed, and broken bits of bone were floating aimlessly in her spinal fluid.

"Get her into the hospital immediately," he snapped as he bolted out of the room.

Sister Andrew raised her eyebrows. "Well, let's get to it."

"Andy! Are you crazy?" Nita responded, incredulous. "This place is fourteen hundred rupees a day! I can't afford that! Forget it!"

They argued all the way back to campus. It's true that Nita's family, back in Sri Lanka, were wealthy, but the Sri Lanka government prohibited the export of money, and Nita's financial support had always been just adequate. A hospital stay could destroy her.

"You have no option," Sister Andrew insisted. "You heard the doctor. You have to get into a hospital. If you can't pay for medical attention here, then I'll put you on a plane back to Sri Lanka."

Within a week Nita could only move by dragging her legs behind her. Under constant pressure from her friend Andy, Nita finally acquiesced. She wearily dictated a cable for the nun to dispatch to the Edwards' residence on Baxter Street in Colombo. It was strangely understated: "Arriving Indian Airlines March 27. Indisposed."

3

Homecoming

Sister Andrew saw to it that Nita was made comfortable
on the plane, carefully strapped to a seat to keep her from
slipping off, but the entire six-hour flight was still a
physical and emotional torment for her. She could see
herself being stretchered off the plane, a crippled martyr,
and her mother collapsing in a nervous heap on the
welcome deck.

Nita closed her eyes, her brow knitted. It was so
degrading, this escapade! The entire thing seemed so
foolish to her—as if she were some tragic clown, strapped
in, dragging her legs around like so much excess baggage.

This was a far cry from the reigning princess she should
have been for her homecoming...a stellar figure, a
glistening trophy of the Edwards family, worthy of her
family name, worthy of her family's applause, a proud Sri
Lankan returning to her homeland in triumph.

It was ironic that Sri Lanka, the beautiful island she
now dreaded to see, was known in literature as "the land
without sorrow, the isle of delight," an island so rich in
natural beauty that legend said Adam went there from

Eden! In fact, the chain of reefs and sandbanks connecting the island to India is still called Adam's Bridge.

In the days of the Sinbad stories, Arab sailors called this tropical land Serendip, from which came the wistful concept of serendipity. Indeed, countless sailors had opportunity to drink in the lush offerings of this fantasy-like place, for the "jewel island" is situated strategically astride the Indian Ocean, and has been a port for the world's seafaring men since before the time of Christ.

Europeans called it Ceylon, and claimed that "from Ceylon to Paradise is a distance of forty Italian miles."

"The sound of waters calling from the fountain of Paradise is heard there," a thirteenth-century traveler wrote.

For the islanders, though, one name has always been adequate for their land: Sri Lanka, "the Resplendent Isle." It is no exaggeration. Luxuriant vegetation covers much of the island, including exotic fruits, flowers, and trees; elephants, water buffalo, sloth bears, and other beasts roam wild; a rainbow of birds make the island their home; wide beaches ring the island nation, and the coastal waters teem with tropical marine life. Warm, wonderful, and waiting are words frequently used in superlatives for the enriched land.

It was the perfect homeland for a girl like Nita Edwards, with such poise and promise. It should have been a perfect homecoming. But no—now the dream was mangled! Her track star's legs hung limply, like mud flaps on a Mercedes. And shame burned in her face when she thought of the sympathy she would be bathed in. It was certainly not how she had imagined herself returning, not even in her most disturbing dreams.

The plane landed roughly, shooting pain through Nita's fragile body, and the passenger exodus began. Nita pushed herself up away from the seat, but it was futile. She was completely lifeless from the hips down. Muscular control had vanished.

The final passenger filed past her, and Nita felt the knot tighten in her stomach.

"Lord, you've just got to get me up and walk me, somehow, off this plane," she prayed silently, fervently, her teeth clenched.

She set the cane aside and lunged forward out of the seat. The numbed legs stood straight beneath her, but atrocious pain gripped her from deep inside and wrenched her breath away.

Flooded by God's grace and pulsing with adrenalin, she shuffled up the endless ramp into the terminal and collapsed into a chair, sweating ferociously. She could not move for two hours, her lungs heaving in and out, desperate with pain. Her jaws ached from her teeth being locked together so hard. Finally she drew herself up and dragged herself step by step to a telephone to call home.

It seemed like hours, but it wasn't long before her mother and uncle arrived. Nita put on a smile and kissed and hugged them. Mrs. Edwards cried uncontrollably but her daughter shushed her with, "Oh, don't; I'll be all right." Nita was following the script she had written in her mind during the jarring airplane ride to Sri Lanka.

Perhaps it was pride that had made Nita set up this homecoming scenario, but, she did not want her family unduly worried. Therefore, she had insisted her family not meet her. She would call them when she arrived. She had brushed aside all offers of help from airline personnel and refused to even consider a wheel chair. Now she was paying for her pride as the pain squeezed the breath from her. Her sheer bulldog tenacity kept her conscious on her hasty ride from the airport to the hospital.

There was a private ward waiting for Nita at Colombo

General Hospital. The family had already watched her struggle to the car at the airport, so now her cousins wanted to pick her up and carry her into the building. But no, Nita insisted she could walk into the hospital!

She crossed the threshold on her feet—defiant. But she would never walk back out. Even her iron will would melt. She was becoming a living corpse.

The last athletic event before the accident

4
The Creeping Death

A concerned doctor smeared plaster down the length of Nita's body, encasing her in a cast from hips down, effectively immobilizing her. The foot of the bed was elevated three feet, tilting her sharply. Then she was weighted with fifteen-pound ingots, to realign her damaged spine. The orthopedic specialist Dr. Shanmugalingham (or Dr. Shan as he was conveniently called) checked her every day. "Three weeks," he assured her, "and you will be all right."

Mrs. Edwards spent day after day by her daughter's bedside. She knew that Nita loved shrimp, so she took to feeding them to her one at a time. Nita could feel the fish travel upward along the crazy tilt of her body, to her stomach, but somehow the fun of munching shrimps soon disappeared.

Hospital aides sponged her every day, dressed her and undressed her, and dressed her again. Each exercise was doubly hard for Nita: each movement sent stabs of pain through her—but it was the incessant invasions of her privacy that rubbed her raw. The daughter of the late magistrate Edwards had never been a hospital patient before, and she had certainly never used a bedpan. Now her biological functions were observed and clocked and analyzed hour by hour. Again and again, Nita's pride was poked and punctured by the crass inquisitions of cold medical science.

Three weeks came and went. Dr. Shan continued his rounds, checking in faithfully every day and talking in hopeful terms.

Six weeks came and went. Dr. Shan kept visiting, but he said less.

More weights were added to the traction unit.

Nine weeks came and went. Dr. Shan missed a day occasionally.

There was no improvement.

Eventually forty-five pounds of weights pulled down on Nita's limbs.

"When am I going back to school?" she asked many times. "I still have finals to take, and they're going to select the hockey team without me if I don't get a move on!"

Beside her bed she kept a stack of fat psychology books. Every day she had her private attendant—a Buddhist girl her mother had hired—stand one of them up in front of her, just within reach of her fingers so she could turn the pages.

She also began exploring the Bible as never before, discovering the Old Testament virtually for the first time. "God is our refuge and strength," she read again and again from Psalm 46:1, "a very present help in trouble."

"Don't study so hard," the doctors would say as they passed by.

"The angle is bad," her mother warned. "You'll hurt your eyes."

Still Nita put in dozens of hours studying, eager to get

out of "this stupid bed," determined to score well on tests she would never take...dreaming of winning hockey games she would never play.

Week plodded after week, fading into a mist of timelessness. A kidney infection took hold in Nita's body, then a urinary tract infection. Elimination became painful, and she began taking medication for each new condition.

Every day she tried to wiggle her toes. She could see them down there, poking through the plaster—but they didn't move at all.

"It's just because of the traction," the doctor insisted. "You'll be all right."

Nita knew that soon the family could inevitably begin thinking of her as a commodity. This fear was amplified when they decided she could get better care in a general ward than in her private ward, because of the more consistent traffic of medical personnel—so she was moved. Hospital policy dictated that private ward patients could have their own linens—Nita's pillow case featured a pussy cat that she was very fond of—but general ward patients could not. The family had to pull strings to get an exception for Nita. By the weight of the Edwards name, and because several of the medical personnel at the hospital were relatives, she got to keep her pussy cat.

The move to the general ward also meant giving up one's private bedpan in favor of the "trolley," a cabinet-like unit stacked with a number of bedpans. It was rolled in periodically for the use of everyone on the ward. Nita was horrified. She cringed at the concept of a dozen bladders being forced to empty themselves on the same schedule, and was aghast at the corruption on the individual bedpans on the trolley. She came to call it "the gallows." But again, her prominent family connections saved her from it. The nun in charge of the ward gave her a brand-new sterilized bedpan, which she could simply turn over to the trolley each time it came around. Nita was still nauseated by the procedure, humiliated by the necessity of a bedpan in the first place!

Nita had no idea how little ground she had actually covered, nor that the worst was yet to come.

She had tremendous confidence in her doctors. After all, she came from a long line of medical people—even her mother was a top surgical nurse—and she knew she was in the competent hands of an orthopedic gold medalist from London. All the doctors seemed keenly interested in her progress, and they were fond of telling her which of her relatives had called after hours the night before to check in on her. When a new nurse joined the staff, one of her first questions was, "Who's this Edwards in the corner that all the doctors seem so concerned about?"

And yet there were gaffes by the hospital staff. One night Nita was snapped out of her sleep by an incredible stabbing pain in her spine. The tension wire on her traction unit had broken—the technician who hooked it up had made an error—and her spine had absorbed the sudden shock.

No other traction unit on the ward ever failed, but Nita's snapped twice more. Each time she screamed with the pain.

"God!" she finally cried out in anguish after the third mistake. "Do you really care?"

Progress failed to occur. There were interminable sweat sessions, as the medical people X-rayed and tested and counter-tested, squinting and sighing and "waiting and seeing."

But there was no improvement.

"God! Do you realize I'm suffering here in this bed?"

A vague new sensation crept in under the plaster one day, and Nita began to complain of a tingling sensation in her toes. The doctors peeled away a little of the plaster and pricked the bottom of her feet with a pin. No response. They pricked the toes, but there was no feeling. Nita's eyes searched the doctors' faces, but she saw no trace of hope.

Day after day, the pricking tests were repeated. After a time, Nita stopped watching their faces and just looked away instead. She felt distinctly like a cadaver being carved and sliced without care or concern, and she could not bear to look at the doctors directly without feeling angry. Her feet bled, soiling the sheets and discoloring the plaster. Nita never felt a thing, except in her heart. There, it hurt.

"God! Do you remember me?"

Three-and-a-half months after her arrival at the hospital, the doctors decided that traction was not helping. The plaster could come off. Nita rejoiced. She imagined how wonderful it would feel to move her feet around again, to flex her legs and stretch and kick and exercise those long-wasted running muscles.

Aides cracked off the plaster in tiny bits. Underneath was the original goopy adhesive, which they washed off with alcohol. Nita could see that her once-brown legs were now a sickly gray-blue.

"Can I move now?" she asked them anxiously.

"Not yet," one of them said. "We have to lower your feet."

They eased the foot of the bed back down to floor level, and Nita could feel the circulation of her blood swimming back down into her legs. After three-and-a-half months her body had adjusted to the awkward upside-down tilt, and now she felt a wave of nausea wash over her. Everything began to look gray, her head felt groggy... and she blacked out.

When she woke up, she was instantly alert. Immediately she tried to lift her knees. They would not move. She tried to wiggle her toes. They lay limp.

"Why can't I move my legs?" Nita asked the nurses around her.

"Oh, you'll be all right," one of them assured her. "We just removed the plaster."

Nita tried again—but nothing.

"The feeling will come back," another nurse told her soothingly. "It may take a little time, that's all. You just hold steady."

The nurses left, but Nita did not hold steady. She poured it on, struggling to make a single muscle move below her waist—to no avail. She lay there completely still, boiling over with frustration, trying to make even the slightest movement, until her neck ached from the tension.

Determined to get answers, she sent for her cousin Robert Benjamin, a specialist who worked one floor above her. He was in surgery at the time, but as soon as he finished he came down.

"Hey, big brother," Nita said, trying to sound light-hearted. "I can't move my legs. What's wrong?"

Robbie looked puzzled. "What do you mean, you can't move?"

Nita shrugged. "I can't move."

He grasped her leg at the knee and ankle and flexed it manually.

"Do you still have the tingling sensation in your toes?"

"Yes, sometimes."

"How's the kidney infection?"

"The same. I'm still taking those pills."

Robbie turned around and walked out without another word. He walked back up to the operating room and found Dr. Shan.

"You've got Nita on that medication for a kidney infection?"

"That's right," the specialist answered, proceeding with his surgery.

"They've stopped using that stuff in England," Robbie went on. "They think it causes loss of sensation."

Dr. Shan looked up momentarily, then back down at his work. "I'll take her off it then. Thank you, Doctor."

"Thank you, Doctor."

Nita looked at her statue-like legs and whispered Psalm 46:1 once again: "God is our refuge and strength, a very present help in trouble." But it was the next two verses that were so hard, "Therefore will not we fear, though the earth be removed, and though the mountains be carried into the midst of the sea: Though the waters thereof roar and be troubled, though the mountains shake with the swelling thereof." She knew it must be true, but she wondered when the strength would come, and when the trouble would end. And it was so hard *not* to be afraid.

The next day was a bit brighter. Nita's sister brought her husband Rex, and a few ladies to visit. They had a good time chatting—it was such a relief to see Nita out of that awful traction!

While the women talked, Rex sat at the end of the bed and impishly pinched Nita's toes. She ignored him. He was not to be denied the satisfaction of a giggle, however. As the conversation went on, he tickled the bottom of her foot. Nita continued talking. Rex's face darkened. He knew something was desperately wrong. Nita had always been ticklish. Now he squeezed her toes one at a time. There was still no response. She had no idea that he was even touching her. She was completely, undeniably numb. The tingling sensation had faded, and in its place was nothing. Nothing at all.

Nita's inquisition continued as the numbness hung on. She had several other relatives working in Colombo General and other area hospitals. Each time one of them visited her, she asked the same questions: "What's wrong with me? Why can't I move my legs?" And to the doctors: "What are you guys doing? When can I get out of here?"

No one came up with any answers.

One day Nita's doctor cousin came to rub her down. While he worked he talked.

"Look, we don't keep you here because we love you and want you near us," he said directly. "You're not doing us any favors by staying here so long. We're just trying to help you get out of here and back on your feet. So you just quit the griping, will you? Shut up, and give us a chance." His voice was flat with frustration.

Nita looked at him evenly. She realized what he was saying by his tone. She was in serious trouble. The implications suddenly occurred to her: she might never be normal again. Instinctively she rushed to stave off the inevitable.

"Please," she begged him, "don't let them send me home in a wheelchair or on crutches. I'll stay a week, a month, whatever it takes to get well. . . but don't send me out a cripple and have the world staring at me and calling me a 'poor thing!' "

Her cousin turned away quickly so she could not see the sting of tears escaping from his helpless eyes.

Nita's fate seemed to be already sealed. She watched as her legs began to warp and bend, and her toes started curling up under her feet. Each day the deformity grew a bit more severe, a bit closer to being grotesque. It was as if she were some horrible wooden puppet being slowly, imperceptibly pulled by some sadistic showmaster.

"Doctor," she demanded fearfully, one day, "How will I run again?"

"It will all work out," he responded softly, feeling no guilt for his lie.

She could see the lights dimming as the parade of medical men dwindled. They were all baffled—she knew that. They didn't want to be reminded of that wall of frustration they could not break through.

And deep within her spirit, Nita felt the creeping dread...the fear that she would never run again, never outrace another tennis ball, never run another 1500. She said nothing, but every day she felt her despair deepening and knew it was the "knowing" that filled her with fear.

When she could no longer feel the icy metal bedpan against her buttocks, Nita knew for sure the doctors were lying. The traction had nothing to do with her toes not moving—her toes would not move because she was paralyzed, and the paralysis was moving steadily upward. She was dying part by part. She touched her legs lightly. They were cold.

Nita continued plaguing the hospital staff and her family for straight answers, maintaining a relentless facade of toughness. But inside she was grieving already for her own demise. She was attending her own funeral. She knew she was in trouble from the day the traction was removed. At night she would lie wide-eyed, straining to move her legs, and watch them lie there, lifeless. During the day she lay in the huge bed, helpless and numb, with her eyes on the door, waiting and wishing for someone to bring the good news—a magic touch—that would restore the old feelings and help her move her legs. But there was no magic lamp and no such genie appeared.

She had trusted the doctors; but medical science had spent its tokens. Dr. Shan stopped dropping by at all.

She bribed a hospital aide to steal the medical records that no doctor would show her. They confirmed the worst.

"God help me," Nita whispered, alone in the night, leaning back on Psalm 46:1. "You are my 'refuge and strength, a very present help in trouble.' God, you are my only hope!"

Vice-chancelor, H.P. university. Dr. Joggi presenting the Inter-collegiate Hockey Trophy (1975-76) last trophy (March '76) in Mandi Valley, Himachal Pradesh

5
Guinea Pig

Dr. Shan had generally visited the ward with an entourage of six or seven doctors and interns tagging along to observe. Now the others began showing up in smaller groups without Shan, probably because Nita's family and friends had badgered the specialists constantly with questions, and they had no answers to give them.

The other doctors had a pattern of callousness. They could not heal her, so they seemed to use her as some human textbook to increase their own knowledge. They normally tested Nita's senses with sharp probes and then stood over her mumbling among themselves. Whenever Nita finally grew irritated enough to ask what they were saying, they invariably ignored the question with a smile, tapped her on the shoulder or ran their fingers through her hair, and said, "You'll be all right." It was the token "concern" that angered Nita most. She could not believe they really cared about anything beyond building their own careers.

They had a way of ignoring the civilities Nita had known

all her life. They would leave the curtain open as they lifted her body and pulled her clothes off, and move her numb legs into a variety of positions, as if Nita had no pride. And always, more pricking with the long needles. They exposed her womanhood without as much as a casual care. She was a sexless mannequin—an object, a thing.

At eleven one morning, one of the doctors arrived with the usual long needle. He put the patient through the usual embarrassing paces, carelessly probing and poking until she was on the verge of exploding. Then, without warning, Dr. Shan strode into the room, with the rest of the group on his heels. He marched directly to Nita's bed, talking loudly, obviously in the middle of some exciting medical discourse to his elite audience. He propped her legs up, pricked her once, and said, "Huh! So you can't *feel*, huh?" And he continued with his speech to the others.

Nita was seething—furious.

As Shan went on talking, he picked up her foot, spreading her legs wide, and began criss-crossing the base of her foot with the long needle. She could see she had become a guinea pig to him, an object lesson for medical students. He kept on talking at full speed, never looking down at the trenches he was digging in Nita's foot. After a while he flopped her on her side and continued his cutting on her thigh, still lecturing with reckless abandon.

Nita's eyes flashed silently; she was irate.

Eventually he went back to her foot, oblivious to his patient, intent only on his own words. Nita felt she was being treated like a cadaver that refuses to cooperate by being considerate enough to die.

A ten-year-old girl in the next bed had watched the entire episode. Suddenly she shouted, "There's blood on her legs!"

Everyone stopped to look at the mess. Nita's foot was

bleeding profusely from the ragged wound. Shan grabbed a wad of cotton and cleaned up the blood and promptly disappeared with his troops. Time to leave the zoo! Nita relaxed her jaws and let the tears brim up in her eyes. The shame, the humiliation, the aching hurt in her soul, was almost more than she could bear.

In mid-afternoon Nita's cousin Chris, a medical researcher, stopped by to visit. He looked at her leg in horror.

"What's this? What *is* this?" he exclaimed.

"It bled today when they tested me," Nita responded softly.

Chris was incredulous. "They're not supposed to test like that!" He stalked angrily out of the ward, hungry for a piece of the man who had carved up his cousin. But his angry attack on the doctor was like closing the barn door after the horse had gone. Nita would bear the scars of that lecture until her dying day.

She closed her eyes, trying to shut out the tension—but it was futile. She felt like a chunk of meat. Her body was numb. Her heart ached.

She longed to go home; to climb out of this white linen casket and back into the comfort of her own house. The house her daddy had built and promised to her. She longed for home, for her old room, for the garden, for the street that led down to the shore, for impromptu cricket matches with the neighbor kids, for her daddy.

6
Fatherless

He had died the day after her thirteenth birthday. Now, as she neared her twenty-third birthday, almost six months after her arrival at the hospital, she thought more and more about him.

He had been one of Sri Lanka's most prominent faces, a man renowned and respected—and rich. He had found wealth in the chambers of the law, and he had built his estate carefully and wisely, as any crafty lawyer should. He was a judge in the city of Batticaloa, where Nita and her brother were reared. He was her father.

Nita loved her father as she would love no one else. He taught her to play tennis and to swim. She had been afraid of the water—she would only put her toes in—until the judge rescued her from everybody's taunting and teasing and lifted her up on his shoulders. Together they strode out into the Indian Ocean. There she was, four-year-old Nita, dangling her legs in the water and kicking and squealing with delight. She wasn't afraid any more; her daddy was the rock. At the end of that day they had to drag her out of the water because she was having too much fun to leave it.

The Edwards were third generation Episcopalians, proud of the Anglican Church, taught to be proper in every facet of life: they were clean, orderly, and educated people—nothing less would suffice. Social graces were high priorities, and the "dignity" of the human being was emphasized.

Nita was engrossed in her education at a proper school on Sri Lanka's west coast when her father had his first heart attack. He was a dynamo, always joking about dying in the harness. "You never know," he used to say with a chuckle, "I might just pop off suddenly someday." And Mrs. Edwards would always return with, "Dad, don't say that. You were a fatherless child; I was a fatherless child. God will never let that happen to our children." But....

He was driving fifty miles to his chambers each day and the pace was wearing. At the end of a typical return trip, he collapsed on his bed, complaining of chest pains. At the hospital, his condition was labeled critical, and the Edwards family flew in all the best cardiovascular specialists they could. Two days later the judge suffered a massive, thumping heart attack. The specialists wrote him off. But he was still in the harness—he refused to die.

For nearly three weeks he hung on. His wife sat by his side nearly around the clock, sponging him and shaving him herself, sometimes refusing even to break away for a shower. She gave him every injection, administered the bedpan, and stood watch at death's door.

Slowly he regained strength.

Very early one morning he began tossing restlessly. His wife got up and walked toward him.

"What time is it?" he whispered hoarsely.

"Two."

The judge smiled. "It's our daughter's birthday, then." In those wee hours, Judge Edwards dictated a cable:

"Loving birthday greetings to darling daughter. May God's sheltering wings protect you and guide you all along life. With love and kisses, Dad and Mother."

Usually Nita had a huge birthday party at the hostel in Colombo where she lived while she was in school. But today there was no party planned. Mrs. Edwards wanted to impress the children with the gravity of Father's condition. Nita's aunt, her mother's twin, was to come by the hostel at nine o'clock the next day to take her home to spend a day with her cousins—a substitute for the canceled party.

At eight, Nita lined up with her mates for daily inspection. Her locker was in order, her shoes were shiny black, and as she stood erect, waiting for the matron, a slashing abdominal pain doubled her over. She dropped to her knees and clung to the bedpost, praying. The pain grew more intense every second for a full twenty minutes, and then finally it stopped as suddenly as it had begun.

Nita waited soberly in the foyer until her aunt came. They drove to her neighborhood and walked toward the house. Coming to meet them was another uncle—not this aunt's husband, but the husband of her father's sister. He had come looking for Nita's aunt.

Nita smiled broadly at him, but he ignored her.

"Hm! The old boy doesn't even greet me!" she teased.

The uncle walked up to them and looked squarely at the aunt.

"They want the children to come home," he said grimly. "The judge is ill."

Nita stopped with a jolt. She knew instinctively—her daddy was dead.

The next hours were like a whirlwind. Nita wept in

anguish, unaware of how she was being transported across the country to her parent's home. Her uncle and aunt tried to walk her up the drive, but her legs refused to function. She could see the big double gates swing open; she could see the many cars in the driveway; she could see that all the lights were on in the house, but she couldn't face any of it. She threw herself into her mother's arms.

"Mama! Why did God let this happen to us?" Her mother was silent in her own sorrow.

Nita was shattered. She cried out for her daddy in her sleep for several nights. She stumbled numbly through the funeral, as her brother Ted stood beside the casket like a block of wood, showing no emotion. Her mother wept constantly and repeated, "Our God could never make a mistake; our God never makes a mistake."

As Nita gained some control in the weeks and months that followed, a taut bitterness drew across her heart. "Daddy's gone to be with Jesus," people told her as they consoled the family. But Nita just sneered inside at the meanness of anyone—Jesus included—who would claim to love her and still take her daddy away. Her family's status meant nothing to her; she had never been impressed by wealth. The comforts of life were conveniences to her, and nothing more. Nothing compared to the love she felt for that man.

Now he was snatched away.

Life changed in dozens of minute ways, all of which added up to grief for Nita. Now her mother walked into the bedroom each morning at six to say, "Time for prayers." Daddy had always sneaked in or hopped in or bounded in. And he always dug up all the bedsheets and blankets and searched for her tiny toes, wiggling them and ho-hoing as Nita giggled. And he always carried her down to the den for prayers.

There were no more hunting trips. Nita always rode on her father's shoulders, carrying the gun, until he spotted the target. He taught her to shoot. Every game she knew, she had learned from him. He was the only person she shared her most precious secrets with.

Now it had all soured. When she heard "God is love," she rankled. It was a ridiculous idea to her. She saw the phrase painted on the wall of a Pentecostal church, and she felt herself flooding with animosity. Her mother took to quoting Romans 8:28, "All things work together for good to them that love God," and Nita grew annoyed by the obvious blasphemy of it. She was alone in the world, and she decided to fight back with bare fists.

To get back at God, Nita began a campaign of deliberate disobedience. When her mother advised her to study, she neglected her studies. Although her mother paid fifteen dollars an hour for tuition, Nita cut classes to catch movies. When she could escape, she ditched church services. She poured herself instead into her sports. If she had a fever and her Mother sent her to bed, she waited until her back was turned and then grabbed the tennis racket and took off to rejoin her crowd of rowdies. And she would stay out as late as she liked, thank you.

Her mother was suffering too, since the judge's death, but Nita had no idea. Now, with Nita rebelling in this way, her mother's heart was shattered. Still, she stood her ground in a quiet way, never forcing decisions on her daughter, only advising as gently as she could. Nita refused it all, and went her own way for three years.

But behind her locked bedroom door, Nita's tough exterior gave way to tears of weakness. She was confused. She did not know how to cope without the foundation her father had provided. And she did not know what to do with the horrible empty longing for peace that she felt every day of her life—a longing she had never revealed to anyone.

Her parents had given her a Bible several years earlier, and now Nita began to read it—suspiciously at first. She noticed Psalm 68:5: "A father of the fatherless, and a judge of the widows, is God in his holy habitation." The description rang strangely true to her.

She began attending various churches in Colombo: Catholic, Presbyterian, Episcopalian, Methodist, Lutheran, Baptist and even Pentecostal. But in every place she found something to sneer at: a misquoted Scripture, an undignified worship format, whatever.

One night, Nita was restless and unable to sleep—unusual for her. She jumped out of bed and decided to raid the refrigerator. She had just stuffed her mouth with good English candy when she heard groaning in another part of the house. She walked toward it and came to her mother's room. The door was ajar, so she stuck her foot in, then her head.

The clock on the dresser read 2:10. Her mother was kneeling at her bedside, her face turned upward, tears drenching her face.

"Lord, I don't ask for fame," she cried. "I don't ask for wealth. I just ask that my children will turn their lives over to you, and live for you all the days of their lives. Please save Nita."

Nita's stony sixteen-year-old heart began an inexorable melting. She tiptoed back to her room, the chocolate having gone tasteless in her mouth.

But the Holy Spirit was quietly at work from the outside as well. A group of Pentecostal young people kept bugging Nita to attend one of their monthly youth parties. She always said yes and then failed to show up. Pentecostals were not her cup of Anglican tea. This loud-mouthed hallelujah shouting was a bit barbarian as far as she was concerned. Nita preferred dignified worship.

The invitations kept coming, though, and finally Nita resolved to go just once to get the pests off her back. She was surprised to find it a pleasant evening after all. They served cookies and cake at someone's home and showed a movie about a drug addict getting his life straightened out. They sang choruses and prayed—which seemed a little pious to Nita—but all in all they were quite a jolly group and she enjoyed herself.

The love she felt in the presence of Christian young people finally snared her completely. The classic verse of Scripture, John 3:16, hit home one day without warning. Suddenly Nita realized that God loved her enough to give up His own precious Son. . . .

She thought back to her own father's love, and through that comparison she began to realize the magnificence of the Heavenly Father's love. Shaken, thrilled, and filled with awe, Nita determined to take hold of this Heavenly Father and never let go. She dug in to the Pentecostal church that her new friends attended, and within the year she was gloriously filled with the Holy Spirit and baptized in water.

"Father, even if it costs me my last drop of blood," Nita vowed on November 16, 1968, "I will live my life for you."

It was a solemn convenant, but as a busy, enthusiastic Christian, Nita soon forgot all about it. God, however, had placed it on file. It was best that Nita could not see ahead ten years, to the day she would lie scarred and helpless in a hospital bed, when her Heavenly Father would call up that old covenant again.

Nita roused herself from her memories.

That was all so long ago. She was strong and vibrant

then, and she had taken it all so lightly. Now she was a dying cripple cut down senselessly by some strange quirk of fate. It would almost be better to die. But death too seemed paralysed. She was in some strange time warp. Day folded into dreary day and the only thing she really knew was that she was sliding inch by inch into some horrible death—waiting, just waiting.

7
In the Pit

Her digestive system was next to go. She had never suffered from constipation in her life. The slightest spicy recipe could always trigger her digestive process, but now the functions ceased, and gashing abdominal cramps began. Four ounces of liquid paraffin brought no results. Seven laxatives lay in her stomach like rocks.

The paralysis had reached her intestines. Menstruation had stopped—her last vestige of womanhood—reminding her that she was now nothing but a lump of cells that refused to work and had slipped into some crazy Rip Van Winkle trance. She was no longer an athlete, a student, or even a woman. Paranoia began to settle in. Nita pored through medical texts and quizzed her doctor-friends on the sly. She could tell that her family was telling her less and less, and she was driven wild to know more. What she read terrified her, but still she had to know.

Convinced that Shan and his orthopedic boys could do no more for her, Nita demanded to be moved to neurology. The red tape seemed to take forever, and when the

paperwork finally did come through it was early one
evening, after her family and other visitors had left. All the
hospital's specialists left at four each afternoon, so there
was no staff to introduce the new patient in the customary
manner. Nita was wheeled into Ward 46 alone.

It was a pit.

Ward 46, the neurology ward, doubled as the emergency ward at Colombo General. Critical cases were
admitted here, then transfered to other parts of the
building. The twenty-bed ward always had about thirty-
five people in it, with patients lying in every crack of space,
even along the outer corridor under a veranda! The
concept of privacy was laughable, even with the bamboo
mats that rolled down from above to serve as curtains
between beds. The walls stopped short of the ceiling, and
crows were common visitors in the rafters. Flies buzzed
and lighted everywhere.

The ward nurse had just come on duty when Nita
arrived. She had no idea who this girl was, or where to put
her, and had not received instructions to move any other
patient out into the corridor, and leave the new one inside.
So Nita ended up in the corridor, not far from the toilet.
The nurse went about her work, trying to care for all the
patients at once.

Nita's senses were already thoroughly assaulted; her
emotions were stretched to the snapping point, and the
scene overwhelmed her.

Visitors customarily used the other side of the corridor
wall for spitting. Nita was not in a position to see this, but
she recoiled in horror every time she heard it. Bloody
emergencies were carted in and out at irregular intervals
and doctors, nurses and visitors squeezed through the
crowded ward incessantly. The horrible trolley came
around. Nita's private attendant squirmed and pleaded;

because of the continuing kidney infection, she was to keep her patient on schedule. But the trolley was filthy, the bedpans on it were grimy, and Nita refused to empty her bladder.

Adjacent to Nita's bed was another holding an eighty-five-year-old woman, who was suffering from dysentery, and who was often completely delirious. The old woman began throwing her stained, filthy bedclothes out of her bed, and they were landing dangerously close to Nita's feet. Nita, terrified, could not even draw up her legs to avoid the missiles of human excrement.

The flushing of the nearby toilet made Nita nervous and she couldn't stop listening to the soft consistant pings as flies ran into the tall metal locker next to her bed. The sound made her flesh crawl. She finally drew herself, as best she could, into a distant corner of her bed and pulled the sheet completely over her head to shut out all the filth. Her mind was racing furiously, her head throbbing and pounding. She squeezed her eyes shut and gritted her teeth, trying desperately to separate herself from the horrors of Ward 46.

Meanwhile, her visitors continued to show up at old Ward 3 and were being redirected to 46. Each of them came to the new location, but no one could see Nita in the outer corridor. Each one in succession left the hospital, puzzled. In her most horrible private hell, Nita was all alone. There was a terrible irony of the evening. The young man who had led her to the Lord arrived with some friends. They had searched all over and finally found her. Nita was fuming.

"Go get my mother," she said sharply.

They left, but Mrs. Edwards failed to show up. She felt a growing terror. Had her own mother turned? Was she so horribly obnoxious now that even her own mother could not stand to see her any longer? Night fell slowly, and finally the ward's main lights were shut off. Hours passed and Nita shivered under her covers.

After a little while, when all was quiet, Nita slowly pulled the sheet away from her head. She gasped. Above her was a grotesque deformed face, gaping at her, slobbering crazily in a toothless grin. She learned later that he, a mentally ill patient in the next bed, had climbed over the metal locker to see what the new girl looked like. Nita choked back a scream and pulled the covers again over her face.

"Go away," she groaned anxiously from under her cover. Then she looked again, and the ugly old face was still there—he just kept staring. Normally Nita would not have reacted to a deformity, but now her nerves were jagged and she could not absorb any more.

An attendant came hurrying back from supper to pull the crazy man back into his own bed. Nita shivered and closed her eyes again.

How much more can I take? she thought. She had to get out of this human junkyard. She would rather be dead than stay here.

The neurological specialist arrived with his staff early in the morning. Nita was already awake. In the morning light her terror had turned to fury. She heard the doctor talking but did not pull the sheet away from her face. Suddenly it was stripped off, and the surprised doctor was looking down at her. He had expected to see a corpse, not Nita.

"What are you doing here?" he cried, not waiting for an answer. He wheeled on his staff. "Why did you put her out here?" he demanded.

They scurried into action, moved another patient out of the room, cleaned the area, and wheeled Nita in.

The doctor checked for output of fluid. There had been

none. He threw back the bedsheet, to find Nita's abdomen looking like a small igloo. A bedpan was called for—sterilized at Nita's insistence—but her system refused to function. The delay had caused complications. The doctor ordered an ice bath but it produced no change. Finally she was hooked up to a catheter.

Angry and aching, she watched a crow take position on a rafter just above her and proceed to drop on her. It was the crowning blow for the daughter of the late Judge Edwards!

She had reached the limit of her calm. When her mother arrived later, Nita's months of bottled frustration finally exploded forth. She attacked from the moment her mother walked in.

"You don't care! Where were you last night? I spent the night in the corridor! You leave me to rot in this stinking place!" The tirade went on.

Mrs. Edwards was shocked. Her brother, Nita's uncle, had died yesterday, and she had raced to arrange the funeral. She had sent a message to her daughter but Nita hadn't received it. Neither had the boys who carried Nita's terse message the night before been able to locate Mrs. Edwards.

Nita's mother had visited her twice every day for more than six months. She had thought that one evening without her would make little difference, and she knew there were several friends planning to visit. She also thought the new ward would be as acceptable as the last, and she knew the private attendant would be on hand.

But she had not counted on Ward 46!

"You are moving me out of this place today," Nita commanded. "I want a private ward."

Visibly upset, Mrs. Edwards walked directly to the front office and filled out the transfer papers. But she returned with bad news. The private ward was being repainted, and Nita could not move in for another twenty-four hours.

Nita sighed, grim-faced. One more night! Well, it couldn't be as bad as the night before had been. But she was wrong. It was a more horrible ordeal than that of the night before—a strange dance of death.

During the day a nineteen-year-old girl was wheeled into the place next to Nita. She was a leukemia victim, the daughter of an undertaker. She had gone home for the weekend but came back critically ill. Through the curtain Nita could hear the commotion around her bed. She kept asking the nurses what was happening, but they told her nothing. Eventually the commotion ended, but the curtain remained down. Nita suspected her wardmate was dead.

Night fell again on Ward 46, and the room grew quiet except for the intermittent groanings of its inhabitants. The private attendant noticed tiny bedbugs crawling on Nita's legs and began picking them off, trying to be casual about it. She knew her mistress would be horrified. Nita noticed—and grew nauseous. She could not even feel the bites, and yet the filthy creatures were growing fat on her blood. Her spirits sank to a new low.

Soon an aide came into the ward and wheeled one of the patients out. There was a sheet over the entire body. Nita shivered and thought of the body that still lay next to her bed. When would they remove that one?

Suddenly the ward exploded into action. Lights flashed on and nurses began shouting and scurrying. A stomach pump was rushed in. A woman had swallowed pesticide, trying to take her life, and was wheeled into the room of broken bones. Doctors and nurses worked her over noisily, until she could vomit on her own—which she proceeded to do throughout the night.

Again Nita felt anger stirring within her. Here, all

around, were people desperate to stay alive, and this cowardly woman creates a ruckus trying to kill herself!

Once more the ward settled down, but before long the night nurse had drawn the sheet over another patient's face. Nita watched nervously as the covered corpse was wheeled past her. She tried to relax, but her heart was beating much too fast for that. As she stared aimlessly around the dark room, the night nurse covered another fresh corpse and signaled for the aide to fetch it.

Nita's heart pounded harder.

Am I next in line? she asked herself frantically. *Will they pull the sheet over my face and wheel me away and dump me in the morgue with the rest of the corpses?*

She had never been exposed to death. She could recall that once her father pulled the car to the side of the road when a funeral passed by. That was all. Her father's corpse was too familiar to qualify as an object of death; she had kissed him, in fact, at the funeral. But now she felt the fear of death taking hold of her. As each new body was removed, she could see death's steady advance.

Yea, though I walk through the valley of the shadow of death. . . . She had learned the verse as a child. Now Nita's mind began to reel with it. She was lying in a death station, waiting for her number to be called.

. . . I will fear no evil: for thou art with me.

It was as if the undertaker were pacing the hall outside her door, waiting impatiently for her. Any breath could be her last. What would become of her?

She breathed deeper, quoting the psalm over and over, but her head kept spinning. The room began a slow, uneven whirl, and through the sickening motion Nita watched yet another whitesheeted corpse slipping toward the exit.

Will I meet God this night? she found herself wondering. *Am I ready to present myself to the Almighty?*

The room spun faster and faster, till it was nothing but a pearly blur; and against the blur she began to see the scenes of her life, flashing in rapid succession...every wasted dollar, every convenient lie, every cherished happiness, every lost friend. She saw her daddy, grinning and joking...her mother offering such strength...her brother and sister in good times and bad.... She saw the rebellious years all over again, incident by painful incident, played out on the movie screen of her memory. She tried to look away, but the movie stayed in front of her eyes. She could hear her pulse in her ears, growing louder by the minute, till she thought her eardrums would burst. And still the memories continued rolling.

Deep into the night, far into the darkness of early morning, the pictures kept flashing before her, until finally they faded. Nita was devastated. She had never confronted much of her past. She had submerged most of it.

In the waking light of morning, against a cheerier backdrop of singing birds and a pleasant breeze, Nita's eyes ran down the lines of Isaiah 43:18, "Remember ye not the former things, neither consider the things of old."

Suddenly she heard weeping from the vicinity of the next bed. The mother of the nineteen-year-old leukemia victim had arrived just as a nurse was yanking the oxygen equipment carelessly off the girl. She had also died long before in the night, like the others, but someone had failed to advise the family.

"Behold, I will do a new thing," Nita read in the following lines. "Now it shall spring forth; shall ye not know it?"

She listened as the body was covered and dumped over onto the death trolley, accompanied by the sobs of a sorrowing mother. Nita thought of her many sins, all dredged up again last night, and how she deserved to be on that trolley. But the Word of God told her differently:

"I, even I, am he that blotteth out thy transgressions for mine own sake, and will not remember thy sins."

Nita felt the soothing ointment of Scripture enveloping her spirit, and she resolved once again to give her life wholly to God.

But the life she was offering to God today was not the same life she had known. Now she began to realize that these memories—the pains and passions of her past—were the sum of her life as a normal girl. There would be no more of them. Her crippled body afforded her no more of that former carefree existence.

From now on, it was the bed, the ward, and—someday, she knew—the grave. But her life, or what was left of it, was God's. It wasn't much, but it was all she had left.

8
Window on the World

When she began choking on her food, Nita's diet was reduced to broth, juice and pudding. She had always loved to eat, but an electromyograph (EMG) showed the paralysis was still advancing upward, now overtaking her swallowing mechanism. A low-grade fever set in. Then, as she watched it helplessly her left hand began to grow cold. Another EMG confirmed that her hand was also paralyzed.

Nita fought off the overwhelming misery by putting her right hand to constant use. She insisted on combing her own hair, brushing her teeth, buttoning and unbuttoning her shirt. She read the Word with a voracious appetite, propping the Bible on her stomach and turning the pages with her right hand. Her exterior was cheerful and visitors found her to be talkative and jovial. She never expressed her fear to anyone, but inside, the fear was very cold and very real.

Nita's roommate in her new ward was a little old lady who was dying of rectal cancer. Nita watched her wasting away and found herself wondering, *Are we under the same cloud of death?* Each day the question seemed to loom larger in front of her.

Her cold left hand became deathly pale, and soon she could not move it at all. The wasted muscles began shrinking, and the hand slowly curled up.

The physical therapists still paraded in and out, going through their assorted charades, twisting and squeezing and flexing the numb limbs. Nita cross-examined each of them, searching for clues about her future. They all said the same meaningless, "You'll be all right"—except one. Roy was a devout Roman Catholic, a father of children who were similar to Nita in age and personality. Watching Nita deteriorate was hard for him. Doctor and patient were fond of each other; they talked comfortably, and Roy never expressed his sense of sorrow or mourning. But neither would he lie to Nita, and when she asked about her future, he always had to say he wasn't sure. She knew he was doing his utmost for her. But she could see his eyes cloud up, and she knew from his face that she was dying piece by piece.

Her sensitivity was vanishing fast. From somewhere along her rib cage downward, she had lost all feeling. When the nurses washed and powdered her, they rubbed cream into her skin. She didn't feel a thing. Each day the paralysis crawled a little further, creeping up her trunk to her shoulders.

Her right hand, still functioning, grew weaker by the day, until it became a chore for Nita to flip the switch on her stereo or pick up her Bible. The attendant's call button was just under her right arm so that when she felt like reading she could push the button and have the attendant put a pillow on her chest, then place on top of that a cleverly designed book stand her cousin had shipped in from England. On that would be placed her Bible.

Little problems grew big as the paralysis increasingly

complicated Nita's life. There was an ancient two-bladed fan in the ceiling over her bed. It was worthless, so her family brought in two new fans, one for either end of her bed. Invariably the breeze would flip the page over before Nita had finished reading it, and she would either have to skip ahead arbitrarily or begin the process all over again by pressing the call button and summoning the attendant for help.

But Nita clung tenaciously to the Scriptures. It was a far cry from her days at the university in India, when she read a few verses out of duty every morning before jogging off on her usual four-and-a-half-mile trek. Jogging now was nothing but a frustrating memory—now, she was literally feeding on the Word, reading and rereading Psalms, Isaiah, Jeremiah. . . .

And visitors continued streaming in and out. Nita was never without attention and affection. On her birthday, as she struggled to keep her mind off her father's death, her room had been steadily engulfed in flowers. First they covered the night stand, then the locker, then the edge of the bed. Finally another table was pulled up alongside the bed, and when it was filled, a second table was brought in and filled. At the end of the day, when everyone had gone, Nita folded her hands, inhaled the fragrant air and said to herself, "This is what I'll look like when I die."

One of her favorite visitors was Father Shirley Ferdinando, a forty-year-old Catholic priest who served the hospital as chaplain. Judge Edwards had strictly taught his children to respect anyone, Catholic or Protestant, who served the Lord. The judge had served as legal advisor to the Roman Catholic priests, and they were often to be found in the Edwards' home, rocking little Nita on their knees. At that time, her parents had a running argument about Seventh Day Adventists: Mrs. Edwards thought they were a cult and should be avoided, but the judge declared that anyone coming in the name of the Lord should be welcome in their home and treated with respect.

When Father Shirley walked by on Nita's first night in the hospital, she had greeted him, partly out of respect for his position and partly out of loneliness. She was, after all, an alien, never having spent time in any hospital before, and having been out of Sri Lanka for the past five years for schooling. Each day as the priest came through to serve communion to the Catholic patients he stopped to chat with Nita. With Shirley's warm sense of humor, they soon became fast friends.

"Hey, how come you pray for them every day," Nita chided him lightly one morning, "but you never pray for me? Come on, pray for me too!"

Shirley blinked in surprise, then closed his eyes and began to pray. Praying for his new friend became part of his daily pattern. The friendship grew stronger. As he met each member of Nita's family, as he heard the pieces of her story, as he learned that her birthday was the anniversary of the judge's death, he was drawn more and more into the circle of her tragic new life.

The chief neurophysician, E.V. Pieris, disliked Father Shirley. Pieris was a Buddhist, fervently anti-Christian, and quick to run the priest out of Nita's room whenever he noticed them together. This girl had entirely too many people praying for her, Pieris grumbled to the staff. Nuns, relatives, now this priest.... If Shirley was going to spend so much time with her, the physician sneered, Nita Edwards might as well be transfered to a church.

But it was Father Shirely who gave Nita a window on the outside world.

She had stared for so many hundreds of hours into the ceiling that she had counted and memorized every slat and

bolt. Dr. Shan had long ago confiscated her collection
of psychology texts—"Bad for your eyes," he had
insisted—and dumped them in the trash. Perhaps this was
an act of revenge for the professional grief Nita had
brought him. With no television on the island, and having
absorbed her limit of varied other reading materials,
Nita's mind had finally bogged down. When she was
alone, a million thoughts crowded each other for attention, but she could concentrate on none of them. Only
visitors set her free.

"Hey, Shirley, guess how many bolts there are in that
ceiling," Nita offered playfully one day.

The priest gaped skyward with his usual active sense of
humor. But the girl's situation hit home with him in that
moment, and he looked around the room for some way to
cut her loose from her prison.

There was a beautiful wooden dressing table against the
wall, with a wood-framed oval mirror attached. Shirley
leaned into it and pushed it toward Nita's bed.

"What are you doing?" Nita exclaimed, as she heard
the noise.

"I'm going to let you see what's going on outside these
four walls."

The considerate priest pushed the dressing table until it
sat at an angle to the bed, then tilted the mirror down by
inches until she could look into the mirror and see out the
window.

It was only a portion of the hospital parking lot—but it
was like the Garden of Eden to Nita. Here for the first time
in months was a window on the world outside, a new sight
on which her weary eyes could feast. And an ever-chang-
ing scene!

Soon her family and friends had found the magic spot
on the parking lot, and they began parking there when

they could, or walking by and waving on their way in to see her. On their way out, too, everyone stopped to wave good-bye. Nita was unable to raise her hand enough to wave back, but, if she gave a big smile they could tell she had seen them.

The physical decay continued, unwilling to be arrested. Week after week the functions of her body broke down, her systems dissembled themselves. Nita's mother, and her family and friends, watched helplessly. Breathing became a tougher task every day, until finally her diaphragm collapsed, another victim of the ghastly paralysis. She began waking at odd hours, choking and gasping for a simple breath. Respiratory emergencies struck with such alarming frequency that an oxygen unit was finally left in her room. To keep her once-athletic lungs from collapsing, she was propped up on a bedrest with ten pillows.

Tubes were poked into Nita's wasting veins, up her nostrils, and down her throat. The constant smell of blood made her sick. She came to dread looking toward the door, for she could see the approach of the laboratory technicians—"the mosquitos," she called them—who came to draw blood samples from her limp arms every day.

There were endless X-rays, endless tests. At a given hour every afternoon she was wheeled down the hall for electrotherapy. There, technicians hooked her up to electrodes and sent jarring bolts of electricity through her body. She arched and jumped with every jolt, but after the session her limbs were always as dead as ever. Her rich-colored skin faded to grocery-bag brown. Her eyes sank deeper and deeper into her skull. As each new organ failed, the pain increased. In tragic irony, the numbness on her exterior was matched inch-for-inch by the physical agony internally. Medication accomplished little.

She took comfort in the Word. Isaiah 43:2 reassured her:

"When thou passest through the waters, I will be with thee; and through the rivers, they shall not overflow thee: when thou walkest through the fire, thou shalt not be burned; neither shall the flame kindle upon thee."

Still, the paralysis crept upward.

The real nightmare had not yet begun.

The miracle was nowhere in sight.

PART II

... And also upon the servants
and upon the handmaids in those days
will I pour out my spirit.

Joel 2:29

Nita, the cripple

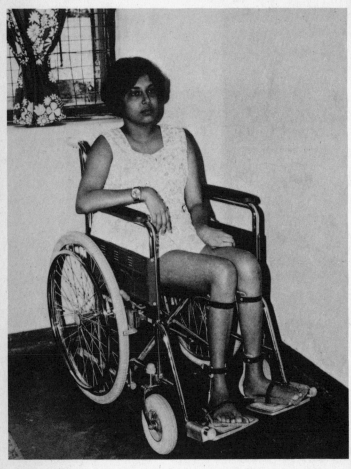

9
The Eighth Face

Nita was in no mood for company. Another in the endless series of tests had just been completed—a lumbar puncture, which was very painful—and furthermore the nurse had accidentally cut her with a surgical knife. After patching the wound they had wheeled Nita into radiology for another in the also-endless series of scannings, and then trolleyed her back to her ward. It was always awkward, trundling her limp body from the rolling cart back into her bed, but today the aides had struggled more than usual, and had bumped her spine on the railing. Nita felt like crying—in fact, loudly,—but she still refused to give in to it.

She lay sulking in the bed, a bag of bones, praying, "Why me, God?" and angrily holding back the tears, when the husband of another relative walked in with Colton Wickramaratne. For a long time he had wanted Colton, his pastor, to pray for Nita.

Nita made every effort to be pleasant, as always, as they were introduced, but she was not disposed toward socializing at the moment. She was still mad at God. She answered the preacher's questions, smiled sweetly, and closed her eyes as he prayed. As he left she said, "Thank you for coming," but she really meant, "Thank you for going."

As a matter of courtesy Colton returned once a week. He normally did the same for anyone in the hospital. He prayed for this young person's healing, and shared the Word with her. Occasionally he would drop by twice in one week, but Nita was never more, or less, enthusiastic than before. She had scores of visitors, and as her condition deteriorated she tired easily and they wore her out faster.

She said she was Spirit-filled, but Colton wondered about that. She never prayed aloud with him, never said hallelujah, never responded with much more than a nod or a pleasantry. Colton had prayed for hundreds in his lifetime; he had seen cancers cured, heart problems solved, and even more dramatic healings of life and limb. But with Nita, he felt he was getting nowhere. At times Nita would grow impatient with his childlike faith. Indeed, she could see that none of his faith-talk was slowing the decay of her body, so she analyzed his statements, piece by piece, challenging him to answer her skepticism. Colton grew impatient too. This wasn't just spare time he was spending, after all! He was a busy man. His church was in a big building program. He had dozens of others to visit and counsel, and the hospital was a good distance from the church.

Colton was always pleasant and polite—so was Nita—but each day as he left, he simmered a little hotter. He could hardly understand her Episcopal decorum since he himself worshiped passionately in the typical freewheeling Pentecostal style. And Nita, after ten nerve-racking, exhausting months in the limbo of paralysis, was not inclined to humor any preacher's peculiar mood swings. Their plastic smiles hid a small hostility between them.

Finally one day, as he walked out of the ward, Colton decided he had dawdled long enough.

"Father, it's a waste of your time," he began in prayer as he walked down the hall. "She's a brick wall. I can't get through. She won't exercise a bit of faith. She will not even say hallelujah."

He walked out the door and toward his car. "It would be different if I had nothing else to do," he grumbled.

Colton got into the blue Volkswagen and slammed the door. "I'm not coming back to visit this girl any more. I've had it with her. Who does she think she is?"

He revved the engine angrily and turned around in the seat to back out of his space, but something unexpected caught his eye. In the window a few paces behind him, he saw a face—*Nita's face.*

She was looking into her mirror, smiling pleasantly, onto the parking lot as she always did when a visitor left. Colton stared hard. He knew it was Nita's face, but somehow it was different. He had seen it somewhere before. He slumped back into his seat and cut the engine.

His mind drew back to that day, twenty years ago, when the eight faces appeared on his wall. He recalled each man's face, and he recalled meeting each of the seven.

But the final face, the woman. . . .

Colton's heart began thumping.

"God, either you're making a mistake, or I'm making a mistake.

"It can't be," he prayed nervously. "That's the face I saw in my vision!"

He sat stunned, and then arousing himself after a final look, he started the Volkswagen. He pulled the car into gear and dashed out of the parking lot, headed for the ocean. He raced to his usual place, his rocky hideaway, and cried out to his Father.

"That girl can't be the eighth face. That girl was only four years old in 1957 when I saw the vision!" he argued with God.

Deep into the night, Colton was still petitioning. "How can she have a role in the Asian revival? She doesn't accept anything on faith! She analyzes everything."

Till two in the morning Colton sat in his hideaway wrestling with God. The sea crashed on the rocks nearby with insistent faithfulness.

"No God, she never even says hallelujah!"

But the conviction would not wash away with the tide, the Lord's answer was simple and direct.

"She is the eighth face!"

Colton dragged himself home, in the early morning darkness. His wife Suzanne and their sons had come to the hospital searching for him, and Nita had told them he had left around six o'clock. They were afraid his car had crashed and that he was lying helplessly in some foresaken ditch. They had called the police and spent the night praying tearfully for his safe return. But Colton had been so shaken in his spirit he totally forgot his family's concern for his safety as he spent the hours in passionate prayer.

Colton came home a different person. His eyes were red, but gleaming. He had had a new touch from God, a new hope for Nita's future—and the future of all Asia. By some miracle, this hopeless paralytic girl was going to be an instrument of revival in Asia. And now, finally he, Colton, could declare his vision! He could share the fascinating promise of God with each of the eight people.

The thrill of his discovery, however, soon wore off.

Colton arrived at the hospital early the next morning with Suzanne and unloaded the entire story...the collection of faces on the wall...and the part that each of these eight people was assured of playing in the Asian revival.

Nita was unimpressed! She was dying of myelitis, a creeping paralysis that was destroying her limbs and vital organs, and, apart from that, she had always been cynical about visions and dreams and voices. The story Colton told her really bore no relevance to her.

"God is going to heal you," Colton insisted. "You're going to have an impact on all of Asia."

"You can't be sure of that," Nita replied coolly. "I come from a family of medical people. I know full well that my disease will eventually reach my heart and lungs, and I will die. But you're good to try and encourage me."

"I would never give you false hopes," Colton answered. "But I *saw* your face in the vision. You are going to live."

Nita shrugged. The preacher could believe whatever he liked. She couldn't stop him.

"I don't expect anything of you," Colton finally said before he left. "I just want you to know what I believe about you, and how I care about what happens to you. I believe God has a purpose for your life, and He wants Suzanne and me to stand with you."

Nita said nothing. He wasn't even her pastor and he was a little too emotional to please her. But if he wanted to believe, that was his business. He would learn soon enough that her case was hopeless.

Colton promised to return. He had to counsel a young couple across town that afternoon, but he would come back the next morning to pray with her.

God had a different agenda.

10
Emergency Call

He dropped Suzanne at the house and drove toward the couple's address. Colton had never met them, but he had promised to stop by their apartment and counsel them about their marriage problems.

"Turn around," the Lord said to him, in a strong inner impression as he drove. "Go back to the hospital."

"But why, Father?" Colton inquired. "I just came from there."

"Nita will need you."

Colton drove on. "Nita has electrotherapy every day at this hour. She won't even be there if I go back," he reasoned with himself.

The Lord kept prodding. Colton tried to ignore it. Maybe he was just imagining things. After all he had just come through a tremendous emotional experience in seeing the eighth face.

He arrived at the couple's apartment and knocked on the door.

"Go see Nita," the Lord insisted.

"Father, that's impossible," Colton protested as he waited for the door to open. "This young couple—I've just knocked on their door!"

"Go now."

"Father, I've promised to see them. They'll have tea and cakes lined up. It's Sri Lankan custom!"

"Go."

"Please come in," the woman said.

In the next split second Colton considered his options. He could ignore the silly notion of driving clear across the city to the hospital, and that would solve his probelm. But no, he had dealt with the Lord too long; he knew better. If he said, "God spoke to me outside your door," these two people would probably think he was crazy and he would never get to counsel with them.

"I've just had an emergency call," he stammered. "I have to go to the hospital."

"Have some tea before you go," the young man offered as the preacher backed away.

"No time, even for tea," Colton blurted, picking up speed. "I'll see you another time," he called over his shoulder. "Make another appointment!"

He ran to the Volkswagen and sped away. Clear across Colombo he gripped the wheel. Something within him had begun to pulsate. But he couldn't tell what was going to happen. The traffic was terrible. Why couldn't all these people get out of the way? "Hurry, hurry," the inner voice said.

Colton screeched into the parking lot and bounded toward Nita's room. Suddenly he slowed to a walk. Nurses and aides were buzzing all around.

He relaxed, "Well, they must be taking good care of her."

But something about the scene, the faces, suddenly

triggered panic in the little preacher. He pushed aside an attendant and peeked into the room. He was shocked. Nita lay crumpled at one edge of the bed, almost past struggling for breath. She had fallen from the bedrest as the nurses transferred her from the rolling cart. Now they were trying to pull her back up, but her gasping convulsions kept them from getting a solid grip on her.

Colton ran toward them. "Get the oxygen!" he shouted as he leaned over her taking charge over the surgical staff. "Call the doctor. Now!" he yelled.

"It's too late," the head nurse answered evenly, with the Buddhist reverence for death. "She is dying." For her, the only proper thing to do was to stand by and let the spirit depart from the body in peace.

Colton didn't answer her. Inside he began screaming, "No! Lord! You told me just last night this woman's witness will bring revival to Asia! I will not let her die!"

Colton pushed the nurses away and lifted up her convulsing body. He dumped her back on the bedrest and then held onto her, praying loudly, rebuking Satan, and crying out to God to spare her life.

The Buddhist attendants watched fearfully from the edges of the room. This strange man with the strange words must be a witchdoctor, for surely he was chanting over the sick one. They were afraid.

For over two hours Colton prayed. Nita's convulsions abated and she lay like a corpse, unconscious and unresponsive. But slowly, smoothly, she began the journey back. Deep in the recesses of her spirit, she heard the distant prayers of a man who loved God. The words floated in and soothed her, like a healing balm, and she knew she was not alone.

She blinked slowly and tried to focus. Colton's hairy arms were extended down to her. He was rubbing her neck. His tie was loose and his blue short-sleeved shirt was drenched with sweat. His face and neck were shiny wet. And he was praying in a language she could not understand but somehow she knew it was very special to God.

She coughed weakly, and Colton opened his eyes, still massaging her neck muscles.

"Nita, this is Pastor Colton," he began gently. "We're with you. Jesus is here. Nita, God loves you. Jesus is here. You're coming through. Jesus is here. . . ."

A doctor came in and took Nita's pulse.

"She's all right," he said, trying to reestablish the official authority he and the staff had lost during the crisis.

"I know that," Colton said, and kept praying.

When the crisis had passed and Nita's mind was clear again, the miracle of Colton's return slowly dawned on her. From that moment she could not deny that God had His hand on her life, that He had sent this man to her as a friend and guide. Maybe, just maybe, there was an alternative to death.

But what did God want from her? She couldn't imagine.

Colton bounded like a hungry tiger into action. He began coming to the hospital at least twice a day, early in the morning and again in the afternoon, to visit with Nita; to pray with her; to talk through a Bible study with her and encourage her. Sometimes Suzanne accompanied him, and almost every day their young sons came along as well. Nita enjoyed the boys immensely as they climbed all over her, pinched her and tugged on her deformed toes and giggled and sang songs and told jokes and made funny faces, all trying to entertain her. Colton would drop by in the evenings too, as he visited other patients, and then sometimes later yet, when Nita's family had gone. On many evenings, Colton was the last one to leave.

The cumulative hours of exposure to this strange little loving man and his sweet wife drew them into Nita's heart, and Nita into theirs. Week by week, she gradually opened up, chatting with Colton, talking about spiritual things, sometimes teasing him about his blind faith—but never again in the old combative way. Suzanne often brought homemade broth and fed it to her, easing some of the burden that Nita's mother had been carrying for so long. Nita grew deeply attached to the Wickramaratnes, and the attachment was mutual.

But Nita's body continued its undeniable breakdown. Her left hand had shrunk to a third the size of her right, and her right hand lost its sensitivity now as well. She could hardly stand to look at her grotesque, hooked fingers. She was slowly curling up as her wasted muscles retracted inch by inch as the result of muscular atrophy. Her legs were strapped to boards (called in Sri Lanka calipuers) to keep them as straight as possible, but it was obvious the splints wouldn't work forever. She had to clear her throat constantly as the paralysis seeped into her neck. Headaches became more frequent, increasing in intensity until Nita thought her jaws would sink into each other. Colton spent hours standing next to her, rubbing her head to ease the pain which he could literally feel throbbing through her skull.

Colton and Suzanne often sat with Mrs. Edwards, praying in unity for their dear one, but nothing seemed to help. Nita refused to cry; refused to beg for help; refused to allow saccharin sympathy as her physical form steadily degenerated. Eventually her neck muscles gave way, and her head lurched helplessly to one side. Gasping respiratory attacks struck with frightful regularity. With each new crisis, nurses cracked open the oxygen cylinder and slapped the mask over Nita's face. One day the cylinder jammed and refused to open, as Nita choked and gagged. Colton prayed feverishly. Suzanne watched the nurses struggle with the cylinder as long as she could. Then she threw herself on the convulsing body and pressed her mouth against Nita's. She blew into the constricted throat again and again, until finally the seizure ended.

The end seemed to be coming every day, and the endless waiting took its toll on Nita's mother. Every day, for months, she had taken Nita's hand, looked heavenward, and prayed in simple, hopeful language for her daughter's healing. Over the months, that hand had warped and shrunk and twisted up, and still Mrs. Edwards' prayer was the same. Nita had rarely seen her cry. She had always been a source of strength and courage. But Mrs. Edwards went home every night and wept bitterly, agonizing over her child's condition. Every night, finally exhausted, she fell into a fitful sleep. Her appetite had vanished.

She had grown thin and, to those who had known her for long, gaunt. But Nita never knew the sorrow her mother was battling.

The day came, however, when her mother's prayer of hope changed. In spite of the spurt of faith the little Pentecostal preacher had briefly generated in her, Mrs. Edwards could no longer hope for her daughter's health.

One night, thinking Nita was asleep and would not hear, she took the deformed little hand in her own and looked upward. She whispered, "Lord, I just can't take her suffering any longer. My girl hurts so much. Please take her home. Let her die!" The hot tears fell on Nita's crippled hand and she had heard it all.

But the Lord refused.

11
Deathwatch

Her long, jet-black hair, once a thing of beauty, had become a matted mess. It had been months since she was able to brush it herself, and weeks since she had been able to feel the brush against her scalp when anyone else brushed it for her. She could not even hold up her own head as the brush was applied.

It was a dying moment for Nita as she called for a hairdresser to cut her hair short. She had loved wearing it past her shoulders—now it had become just one more victim of the paralysis. With every snip of the scissors, Nita hurt again. As the disease progressed even the lovely little niceties of life were being cut away.

If anyone could lift her spirits on such dark days, it was Michaele, Colton's youngest son. He was Nita's favorite. The most affectionate of the bunch, he was fond of sitting on her bed, fidgeting and pinching and tickling her, delightedly exploring her areas of numbness. Nita would have been horrified if it had been anyone else, but Michaele was too cute to be anything but engaging.

Tragically, it was Michaele who discovered that Nita had lost all feeling in her face. Nita had known it for some time—when the nurses washed her she felt nothing—and she was especially discouraged by this, for it left her practically a hunk of lifeless leather, with no sense of touch anywhere on her body. She was so deflated by the discovery that she had not even reported this final lapse to the doctors.

Her vocal cords too fell into disrepair, and her voice disintegrated into a whisper. In a matter of days it vanished altogether. Colton resolutely learned to read her lips, and he served as her interpreter when others were in the room. Nita's Buddhist attendant had to learn lipreading also. Yet every turn for the worse seemed to strengthen the bond of love between the preacher and the patient.

It became evident that Nita was dying—evident to everyone, including Nita. She could see, as her mother and others kissed her good-bye at the end of each visit, that they were not sure they would ever again see her alive. Mrs. Edwards was asking more frequently and more frantically these days if there was anyone Nita wanted to see—her brother Ted perhaps? Nita had always said no, don't make Ted fly in all the way from England. But now she finally relented. She wanted to see him at least once more.

The Singapore relatives planned to make their pilgrimage at Christmastime, and Nita's uncle from Zambia was coming in then too. Mrs. Edwards hoped secretly they would not be too late.

Heart problems began as the paralysis progressed. Each attack knocked Nita unconscious, and as she came to she could hear "Hail Mary's" and groanings and smell the antiseptic odors and see the masks and caps and ugly green gowns all shuffling about. One day she woke groggily in the intensive care observation cell, completely alone, surrounded by walls of shiny machines—one monitoring her pulse, another her blood pressure, another her temperature. There was a single metal door with a tiny window. In it she saw an open eye, someone whose job it was to see if she had died yet.

Nita pressed her eyes shut. It was like a gruesome movie, "The Deathwatch," and she was its star.

She had trusted the doctors. They had failed. She had prayed for God to heal her. He had not. In her secret moments, she had even prayed to die. That didn't work either. She had kept up a cool facade, but all the while, inside, her heart was breaking.

"Behold, I have refined thee, but not with silver," she read in Isaiah 48:10. "I have chosen thee in the furnace of affliction."

But why? What did God want of her? What was He doing with her life?

The physical problems accumulated, the emotional struggles multiplied, and finally the spiritual question consumed her. One day, alone with Colton, the wall began to crack, and Nita let herself weep openly. It was the first time.

Colton ached for her, and repeated words of Scripture, and prayed with her, as he had done so often.

"Oh, Colton," Nita sobbed, "why don't you just stop praying for me?"

"No," he replied, adamant. "I'm not going to let go until God tells you what He intends to do with your life."

A subtle change occurred in Nita that day. Her prayer life experienced a fundamental change.

"I'm not asking for healing any more," she told the Lord each day. "I'm not asking to be taken home to heaven. Just tell me what you created me for, and do anything you like with me."

She doggedly repeated the prayer, day after day, night after night.

"If your plan is to let me die, glory to God," she often added, her fear of death completely gone.

"If your plan is to let me lie here like a vegetable for fifty years, glory to God. I don't like it, but I'll live for you right in this bed. Just tell me what you want me to do, why you created me, what purpose you intended when you formed me in the womb. What is your plan for me?"

Almost by the hour, Nita picked up spiritual momentum, even as she physically wasted away. She had renewed her childhood covenant with the Lord—she would give her last drop of blood, her last earthly breath, to her Heavenly Father.

When she felt herself doubting that God would ever answer her, she repeated the last verse of Isaiah 40 as a counter-argument:

"But they that wait upon the Lord shall renew their strength; they shall mount up with wings as eagles; they shall run, and not be weary; and they shall walk, and not faint."

And for Nita, that promise—mounting up, running, and walking—made it worth the wait, even if it would only be a figure of speech.

It was a strange change, after so many months of demanding a miracle of healing. Colton and Suzanne, her mother, and hundreds of Christians all over Sri Lanka, were demanding her healing, and in the swirling midst of all this, she was asking only for a *word*—not action.

And daily, Nita's spiritual pipeline was being cleared. The earthly longings she had felt for so long were being swept away. The obsessions of her teen years, the self-indulgent prayers, the earmarks of immaturity began to be dissolved within her by a divine touch. Every day, she could sense in her spirit that her spiritual pipeline was coming a little closer to a total cleansing—a little closer to the day when it could freely transport God's answer to her heart.

The challenges continued, however, on every level—physical, emotional, spiritual. As Nita read II Corinthians 4:8-10, she saw herself in the words:

"We are troubled on every side, yet not distressed; we are perplexed, but not in despair; Persecuted, but not forsaken; cast down, but not destroyed;

"Always bearing about in the body the dying of the Lord Jesus."

The advance of death indeed appeared to continue in Nita's body. Her eye muscles began to be affected by the disease, and double vision soon made it hard for her to keep her eyes open when the room filled with visitors. The tear ducts failed, and the corners of her eyes leaked salty tears continuously, stinging her eyelids. She was embarrassed. Her visitors were bound to see her tears and sympathize more profusely than ever.

With her vocal cords dead, she could no longer create the lightweight atmosphere that she had always worked for—cracking jokes and teasing her visitors, to make them laugh and feel at ease. The constant discharge from her eyes made her nervous as well. She knew her face was wet, but she couldn't feel the tears.

And now her mirror was worthless. She could no longer see as far as the parking lot. Even the ceiling slats and bolts were beyond her visual reach. To read the Bible she had to have the page held an inch from her eyeballs. The strain was crushing.

Her eyes would do her one final disservice. She had not seen herself in a mirror for many weeks. One day, as she was being unloaded off the cart, she caught a glimpse of herself. A glimpse was all she needed. The picture instantly locked into her memory. She was sickened. She knew she had been pretty—not gorgeous—but she had been satisfied. The girl in the mirror was a wench. Her hair was cut short around her puffy face, badly bloated by massive doses of cortisone. Under her eyes hung great, sunken, dark bags. From her neck down, her skeleton was evident. Her athletic muscle tone had given way to a distended abdomen after months of artificial digestives and a liquid diet. Her hands were all knuckles, her fingers so grossly deformed that they looked like bird claws.

It was this awful creature that Sandy Koelmeyer found in Ward 13.

12
I'll Celebrate

Sandy had grown up with Nita. They were best friends in the classic sense of the term. They went to school and church together, played tennis and hockey together. If Nita was not around the house you could be sure she was at the Koelmeyers' or off somewhere else with Sandy.

The girls had sometimes teased each other about dying.

"You jolly well better come to my funeral *sad*," Nita insisted.

"Oh rubbish!" Sandy always retorted. "I'll celebrate! I'll wear a red dress and say, Thank God I got rid of the pest!"

Now Sandy lived with her husband in Australia. One of their old schoolmates had called her there and told her the medical verdict: Nita was going to die.

"If you want to see her, you'd better come now."

The family decided a surprise of this magnitude might be hard on Nita's weakening heart, but Sandy's brother-in-law Ashley, who had grown close to Nita since her return to Sri Lanka, decided to have a little fun with her.

"Santa's bringing you an early Christmas present," Ashley suggested slyly.

Nita smiled warmly, unable to talk but enjoying the game already.

"And it's a big present. It's five feet tall," he continued.

Nita grinned but couldn't guess.

"Sandy's coming."

Nita's jaw dropped and her eyes rolled around in silent delight. This would be great!

The day came in early December. When Sandy arrived, all the family and friends quickly left the room so the two girls could enjoy their reunion alone.

Sandy came into the room and then paused. They had warned her how bad it was, but she hadn't been able to picture this. She walked close to the bedside and just stood there, frozen.

Neither girl had ever been the type to cry, but they cried together. Sandy couldn't find any words. Nita felt desperate. She couldn't reach out as she normally would, couldn't embrace Sandy as she longed to do. After a short while Sandy sat on the bed and leaned over her friend. In the old days they would have kissed each other, but Nita had so many tubes in the way.

They wept for a long time. When Sandy could finally talk, it was hard. Nita agonized; she wanted desperately to talk with her, to share things with Sandy that she could never share with anyone else. She strained to squeeze her voice out of her throat, but it was hopeless. Sandy had to read her lips; but she wasn't used to it.

Nita grew fatigued. The reunion had to end.

But Nita was eager to see her again, and Mrs. Edwards got Sandy a visitor's pass so she could come and go freely. The next day was better, and the next. Sandy would stay into the New Year. For Sandy, the shock soon wore off.

She kept tissues nearby and mopped Nita's face, and after a day or two they could finally cut loose with each other, almost like the old times. Nita knew she could complain and Sandy would understand. It was the finest therapy.

13
Exit

When Sandy left one day Nita asked her attendant to help her read a few verses in the Bible.

The strangest thought came to Nita's mind one day as she read Isaiah 41:10:

"Fear thou not; for I am with thee: be not dismayed; for I am thy God: I will strengthen thee; yea, I will help thee; yea, I will uphold thee with the right hand of my righteousness."

And as she read further, she was stopped in her tracks by Isaiah 42:6:

"I the Lord have called thee in righteousness, and will hold thine hand, and will keep thee, and give thee for a covenant of the people, for a light of the Gentiles."

If He had promised to strengthen her, to hold her hand, then why not trust Him fully?—leave the hospital and get an apartment?

It was absurd—she was a total vegetable, physically— and yet as she thought about it, Nita felt a deep assurance that this truly was the leading of the Lord.

Besides, she was tired of being everybody's chunk of meat: the doctors would stand outside her door looking at the records and exclaiming their surprise that she was still alive, as if she couldn't hear them, and she didn't need that kind of carelessness any more.

Still, it took her a while to muster up the confidence to tell anyone about the idea. She knew there would be opposition. Her fears were soon realized, and her mother was, by turns, frantic and angry. She had spent thousands of dollars on the finest medical care available in the country, and now Nita was going to jeopardize her very life by moving out. The cousins, uncles and other relatives thought it was ridiculous. Perhaps Nita was losing her mind? Perhaps she was becoming suicidal? Some of them advised simply refusing her. What could she do about it, after all? If no one moved her out, she had no way of leaving.

Only Colton understood.

"I feel God would have me leave the hospital," Nita said to him through silent lips.

"I'll talk to the doctors," he said compassionately.

"Nita feels God is telling her to leave the hospital," Colton told them.

"Well, tell her God wants her to stay here," one of them suggested snidely.

"I can't tell her that," Colton replied. "But if staying is the best thing for her to do, I can tell her that."

"Tell her that, then. It's foolish for her to even think about getting more than a few yards away from the intensive care unit. She's in there every other day as it is."

Colton gently relayed the message. But Nita was prepared. She had not received an answer from God as to the question of her destiny, but she knew a move like this would still give Him all the options, and that was argument enough for her: "If God's plan calls for me to die, I can die in my own place just as well," she explained calmly to him. "There is nothing much to lose. Think of this as my last request. Let me go spend time alone with the Lord, according to my convictions. And, if it is my destiny to live a long life as a cripple, I can do that elsewhere too."

Colton smiled as she approached the third option—his favorite: "And God can certainly heal me anywhere He wants."

She attached two conditions to the request: she wanted an apartment of her own, and she wanted no visitors other than her mother, Colton and Suzanne, and Sandy.

She couldn't think of going home to her own house; it would drain the life right out of her mother. She could move into a single flat with her private attendant and learn to cope.

And she had tired of the gawking. She had been examined thoroughly and constantly by doctors and nurses for over a year, and that was enough. Besides, she had become something of a Christian tourist attraction as people heard about her condition. Every few days another group passing through Colombo would stop by to see her, ostensibly to cheer her up and pray for her—and they inevitably ogled. She had seen herself now, too, and she did not care to have even her relatives seeing any more of what she had become.

Mrs. Edwards stalled. She offered to send Nita to the United States for treatment. But word came back that there was no cure available there either; they could only keep her alive for four-hundred-and-fifty dollars a day, plus medication.

Colton assumed the yoke of the argument on Nita's behalf. He knew she could never argue her case successfully without a voice, virtually without a physical body.

He negotiated gently, firmly, and wisely with the family. Tension filled the room, then evaporated, then returned, as the struggle stretched into days and weeks, to Christmas. But Nita's case was won.

Christmas was a minor tragedy in itself. Family and friends brought expensive gifts which Nita could not open. There was a lot of Christmas candy and cake, and pudding brought from England, which she could not taste. Her room was all decorated with festive Christmas trimmings which she could barely see, and several groups came by from churches to sing carols to her, but she was self-conscious and uncomfortable.

Nita's last night in the hospital, December 30, was like her funeral in advance. All the relatives and friends turned out to cry over her body. They knew they would never see her alive again. She was going into hiding to die.

There were other tensions too. Some of them thought Mrs. Edwards must have decided that Nita would not have any visitors. Others blamed Colton and Suzanne. There would be hard feelings in the family for some time to come. Loved ones and friends felt shunned and hurt. They could not understand that it was a spiritual thing, where God wanted Nita to rely totally on Him.

Nita thought of her old English literature studies at the university. She could still quote a snatch of Shakespeare:

"There is a tide in the affairs of men
When taken at full lead on
But if omitted all of life
Is left in the shallows."

The months she had wasted when she could have been studying now returned to haunt her. She had expected to leave the hospital under much different circumstances, returning to school for more fun and frolic. Instead, she had no hope of ever again leading a normal academic life, the kind of life she had taken so for granted.

Angry at herself, she resolved to find a way to achieve the education she had begun years ago. She would strap herself in a motorized wheelchair and learn to drive a special car—whatever it took—to make good on those squandered opportunities.

As her anger subsided, though, she knew her tide had already gone out the final time. She had not taken it at full.

At the farewell gathering, the nurses and doctors were as red-eyed as the relatives. They had been even closer to Nita in the past months than her family had been. Nita knew what their grim faces were saying.

She was lifted onto a stretcher and lugged down the hallway. As she was carried out the back door of the building, she thought how different it had been the day she first crossed that same threshold. It was backwards, this story of hers: she had walked in, now she was being carried out.

A Red Cross ambulance was waiting to bear her body to its new resting place. Nita could make out its design, and see that it was a hearse, but without the nice decor. As they slid her in, she couldn't help but think, "This is how it will be when I'm dead."

It was an emotional little trip. Her mother and her attendant rode with her. She could tell that her mother was thinking of the last time she had ridden in an ambulance, with her father.

Nita could barely see the tops of trees as the ambulance sped through Colombo's streets, and she knew this could be the last time she would see the lovely little island. Her vision had failed her, but some days were better than others. She was grateful that at least this was one of her better days.

Suzanne had gone ahead. The ambulance pulled into a pleasant little driveway in a lovely yard, and everyone got out to make arrangements for Nita to be brought in. She was alone in the back of the ambulance waiting like an excess piece of luggage forgotten in the trunk of the family car. The neighborhood kids quickly gathered around to look through the windows. They had heard that their new neighbor was a paralyzed girl. This crooked thing must be her.

14
"Flush That Stuff"

It was hard to maneuver the stretcher up the little stairway into the apartment, and Nita imagined how much simpler it was going to be when they moved her corpse back out.

Nita's mother with Colton and Suzanne made her comfortable and then, a little hesitantly, they all left. Nita was alone with her medical attendant, the Buddhist girl.

"Bring me all the medication I have," Nita said immediately, mouthing the words carefully.

The girl was puzzled, reluctant. Nita repeated herself.

She came back with an armload—all the medication Nita had been taking in the hospital. There were pain killers, sedatives, cortisone, Valiums, phenobarbitals—a massive amount of medicine.

"Empty them all in the toilet," Nita told her, "and flush them down."

The girl's eyes widened. She was astonished and afraid. Nita was her responsibility, hers alone. There were no more doctors to call, no bells to ring, no oxygen—nothing.

"I can't do that," she finally responded, still amazed at

the order. She knew what Mrs. Edwards would say when she found out. "Mistress will get very upset with me."

As the girl watched her lips, Nita looked at her squarely. "Now I want you to know something. It's just you and me here, nobody else, and I am the boss. You follow my instructions and obey my orders. Now go flush that stuff."

If God were going to heal her, she did not want medication robbing His glory. If He were not, then why not get it over sooner?

"And furthermore, this is between you and me," she added emphatically. She knew her mother would panic; she was already unnerved about the whole move.

"You dare not discuss this matter with anyone."

Besides, someone was bound to think she was trying to commit suicide. The nurse nervously flushed everything.

Sometime after midnight on New Year's Eve, after the watchnight service at Colton's church, he and Suzanne came to Nita's apartment and gently woke her.

"Happy New Year," Suzanne whispered.

Nita smiled wryly. The new year held no real promise of happiness for her, and the greeting sounded hollow.

Colton served her communion. Then Suzanne spotted the last of Nita's Christmas gifts, still unopened, so she opened them for her with as much gusto as she could engender.

But Nita was a bit somber.

The deathwatch continued. Nita's brother Ted, nine years after leaving Sri Lanka, arrived on a flight out of London, and was met at the Colombo airport by his mother and an uncle. He had always been the essence of calm and good sense, but as he passed through customs, Mrs. Edwards noticed his hands were trembling.

Nita awoke at nine o'clock that evening and focused on a nice-looking gentleman by her bed. Ted had been there for five hours, weeping uncontrollably, clutching her deformed little hand, methodically prying open the crooked fingers, watching them curl up, and prying them open, again and again. As she awoke, he leaned over and kissed her. Nita couldn't help but recall the same brother at her father's funeral, so solemn and sedate, so in control.

She still had the first gift he ever bought her, when she was two—a little piggy whose ears she had promptly chewed up. She and Ted had been good friends. She was a tomboy, and Ted called her his little brother.

He had followed her progress from afar, keeping tabs on her schooling, her growing athletic prowess, her victories, her travels. He had watched from England with pride as she grew into a beautiful young woman. And now he was shattered, as he watched her suffer, listened to her coughing and wheezing. She was wasting away. He hurt for her, more than he had known he could ever hurt.

Life had changed abruptly with the move to the apartment. If Nita choked for air, if her heart stopped, in every emergency, prayer was the only remedy. It was administered in varying doses by Colton, Suzanne, their boys, Sandy, and Nita's mother.

Without the medication, Nita's pain increased, and the attacks came more frequently. Surely her body would soon cave in, just from abuse.

And yet, now, as she lay here alone, hour after hour, the spirit of sadness gave way, and her spiritual pipeline grew clearer than ever before—a beautiful, wide-open channel of communication with her Lord. As she prayed and listened to God, they grew closer and closer.

It was the most splendid fellowship she had ever known, as she unburdened her heart and unleased her sense of self, and He ministered His perfect love to her. It was as if He were her Daddy, back on the front lawn at the big house, and they were talking over some simple childhood problem...something her daddy could solve.

15
Voice in an Empty Room

"When I die, you'd jolly well better be sad!"

"Rubbish. I'll celebrate."

Nita's mind reran the old funny exchange from her teen years as the hour approached when Sandy would have to leave. It was the fifth day of the new year, and they had spent virtually every daylight hour together over the past three weeks, precious times for Nita, considering the circumstance.

Now they were over. Nita felt a heavy load in the pit of her stomach as she looked at her petite friend, so alive and healthy, and so grief-stricken for her. In a way she would rather have died while Sandy was here in Sri Lanka, instead of waiting till she was back in Australia.

But I'll never see her again, Nita realized. As the noon departure hour overtook them, the girls repeated their opening scene, weeping without words. Sandy finally walked out the door, and as quickly the apartment was draped in a spirit of heaviness.

Psalm 31:1 rolled through Nita's mind, as it had many

times in the past weeks: "In thee, O Lord, do I put my trust...deliver me in thy righteousness." It had encouraged her before, and now she clung to it again.

She had leaned on Psalm 91:2 as well: "I will say of the Lord, He is my refuge and my fortress: my God; in him will I trust."

And still she was waiting on the Lord to renew her strength, waiting to mount up as an eagle, waiting for the time when she would run without weariness, and walk without fainting.

But the emptiness—the sense of hopelessness—was devastating as Sandy's absence engulfed the room.

She lay in her misery for four hours, wide awake, unable to escape into sleep. The soft sounds of the afternoon filtered lightly into her upstairs room.

Suddenly, without warning or fanfare, at about four o'clock she heard a voice. It was a man speaking to her in a soft, but authoritative tone. It was the clearest tone she had ever heard.

"Nita, I'm going to raise you up to take the gospel to Asia."

She was startled. If she had been able to, she would have jumped. She had thought she was alone in the room. Where had that voice come from? It said further: "I'm going to heal you on Friday the eleventh of February."

Nita's heart pounded. She was sure no one was in the room. She had never heard that voice before. She felt an uncanny twinge in her spirit. But she knew better than to be fooled into thinking the Lord had actually spoken to her in an audible voice.

She rolled her eyes around the room as far as she could see. The voice had come from behind her, so she couldn't see who was there. But someone must be there!

She struggled for the call button and buzzed for the

attendant. If there was a man in the room, she wanted to know.

Since Nita's voice had failed, the attendant could often guess her meaning by the way she moved her eyes. Nita looked toward the door with a fearful face. The attendant had checked Nita's room for lizards many times, here and in the hospital—they were always crawling into corners, and Nita was terrified of them—so now the nurse proceeded to look for a lizard behind the door. There was nothing there. Nita's eyes moved to another corner, then another, and eventually the attendant had scoured the room. No man nor lizard turned up.

Perhaps under the bed? Nita made the girl get down on her hands and knees and look. But no one was there.

Skeptically, but with excitement slowly mounting inside of her, Nita mentally checked off the possibilities. It could be a dream, but she was wide awake. It could be a hallucination, but she had been off all drugs for several days. It could be her own imagination, but she wasn't even in a good frame of mind—and she knew she had heard a man speak to her, as clearly as anyone had ever spoken to her.

Knowing the extremism of some of her family and friends, it could even be a set-up; someone trying to do her good, give her hope, pretending to be the voice of God—except that the lizard check had ruled out that possibility. The radio was off and there was no recording equipment around at all.

Which left two possible sources: God and the devil.

Nita had never taken kindly to people who proclaimed that God had spoken to them. She had always been suspicious of that whole realm of thinking. To her, even Colton sometimes very nearly crossed the line. But deep in her heart, she already knew she had heard from God; that

He had answered her question; that He was going to heal her on Friday, February 11, and that He had answered her question in a completely unique and thoroughly dramatic way.

Still, she just had to be sure.

So she prayed a hard-nosed, practical prayer:

"Lord, I've heard this voice. If it's yours, I want a confirmation."

She felt suddenly awkward, being so bold with the Almighty Creator who had just promised to heal her and done so in an audible voice. But she thought of Gideon, laying out his fleece, and she decided to press on with it.

"I want to hear the promise again," she prayed bravely. "In public. Let other people hear it too."

It was an impossible request, especially since Nita never left her apartment.

She never mentioned the incident to anyone; never hinted that she had heard from God or that she was seeking a confirmation. But she steadily kept her heart open, worshiping her Lord alone, and with Colton and Suzanne and her mother, for hours on end, day after day.

Colton's schedule tugged him away a little more each week. His huge church building program was drawing to a close, and the grand finale—the dedication of the new church building—was fast approaching. Syvelle Phillips, a major international voice of the Full Gospel movement, was flying in from California to preach the dedication service for Colton's church. It was to be an event of such significance to Colton and his family that they never thought to ask Nita if she wanted to go; instead, they simply presumed it. Nita was unenthusiastic when she heard their plan.

Ted flew a collapsible wheelchair in from England. When it arrived, Colton and Suzanne and the boys unpacked it with giddy excitement. Nita was morose. She had no desire whatsoever to be wheeled into a brand-new church building with fourteen hundred people peering all around. Besides, Colton had requested prayer for her so often and had spent so much time visiting her that she had become something of a joke to the young people of that church—and almost a sore point with some of the older ones.

Colton would not be denied, though, and reluctantly Nita agreed to go. She could not disappoint these people who had been so kind to her for so long. It would mean a lot to them if she would attend.

The boys had loads of fun wheeling themselves around in the new wheelchair, but Nita did not even want to look at it. To her, it was a symbol of what she had become. She could no longer control her body functions at all. The attendant had to change her bedclothes several times a day, like the ritual diaper change on an oversized baby.

"Let's try out this new wheelchair, Nita!"

Michaele pushed her around the garden a few times, then they left for the church. It was a beautiful structure, but Nita could not take much of it in. Colton had graciously arranged for them to arrive early, so Nita could be situated in the choir loft between the piano and the wall—neither Colton nor Nita wanted her to be a spectacle. From her cubicle and with her vision problems, she could see very little of what went on, but in the divine plan she was really only there to hear one thing.

A message in tongues, familiar in Pentecostal services, cut through the service like a knife, arresting the attention of the people assembled there. As the last sounds echoed into the rafters, Syvelle Phillips lifted his voice and began declaring the interpretation. Only Nita had heard the phrases before: "God will raise you up to carry the gospel to all of Asia. His word to you is true. Trust Him. He will not lead you astray. He will glorify Himself through you.''

Nita's heart began to leap with joy. It was true. She had heard from God, and He had confirmed it—here, before fourteen hundred people, honoring her request to hear it in public! The very words God had said!

Nita was ecstatic. Long after the crowd had cleared, she was hoisted out of her little hole. She was still radiant. And in her heart, she felt the assurance of the Lord that there would be icing as well as cake: He would give her yet another confirmation.

It was in this victorious frame of mind that Nita decided to ask for more information. As the nurse changed her bed linen, the next morning, Nita was placed in her wheelchair. She sat by the window, with the sunlight streaming in on the pages of her Bible, and she thought about the day she would be healed.

"Father, you told me the day and the date," she said simply. "Please, don't keep me waiting all day. Please tell me the time too."

She half-expected to hear the voice again, but she heard nothing. Instead, a silent inner voice spoke to her heart: she would be healed at 3:30 in the afternoon.

Nita thought she would burst with excitement. She had the date and the hour now—February 11 at 3:30 p.m. She was going to be healed by the power of God, and she was going to watch it happen!

The next Sunday, Ted decided he wanted to take his little sister to church. Nita didn't look forward to this outing any more than she had looked forward to the last. But Ted was so driven to do things for her that she acquiesced. The dignified accountant had no idea how to carry a cripple so he was helpless trying to get her out of the apartment until Colton's boys, experts by now, came to the rescue. At the church, Nita was positioned in the aisle, with Ted protectively seated next to her.

Suddenly a message in tongues split the air, and again the interpretation rang clearly through the sanctuary. A message miraculously similar to the first one. Nita could hardly believe the great love of her Heavenly Father in giving her not one, but two confirmations.

Nita wept uncontrollably, riveted by the majesty of God. She was embarrassed by her reaction, real emotional tears flooding down her cheeks. She had never cried in public in all these months. She had even waited every night, back in the hospital, until the nurses made their final rounds, before she would let herself cry. But now there was no more doubt in her and she wept with joy. The voice she had heard was her Heavenly Father's. She had waited on the Lord to renew her strength, and soon she would mount up as an eagle, she would walk and not be weary, she would run and not faint. Friday, February 11, she knew without question, she would leave that bed and wheelchair forever, and walk away a free woman.

She wanted to tell the world, but she felt deeply impressed not to share the news with anyone yet. It took a conscious effort to control the urge.

Colton's boys came to lift her away at the end of the service, and Nita knew, as they jostled her down the aisle and out to the car, that it was one of the last times she would be borne like this, like luggage going where someone else wanted it to go.

16
Circle of the Sacred Trust

"What will you be doing on the afternoon of the eleventh?" Nita asked the boys nonchalantly as they settled her back in her wide bed. "Maybe you could come by and spend some time with me." It was still a few days away.

One of them had a class to attend: the other one said sure, he would drop by. Nita smiled and closed her eyes, deeply satisfied. She couldn't tell them what was going to happen, but she didn't want them to miss out on the glorious event she knew it would be.

The next morning Nita's Buddhist attendant began the usual routine of washing and dressing her. While she changed the linens, she again put Nita in the wheelchair near the window, with her Bible on the bookrest on her lap. Nita strained to see the words, but some days it took forty minutes to get through a single verse of Scripture, and today was no different. When the attendant transfered her back to bed she knelt down with her back to the bed to straighten the dresser drawers. Nita looked down at her, and it occurred to her for the first time how long she had spent with this Buddhist lady. Now, in a few days, they would be separated—and Nita had never spoken to her about accepting Jesus Christ as Lord and Savior. The woman had observed plenty at close range: people had prayed hundreds of times in the hospital and the apartment; Nita had spent hours in prayer, and more hours reading her Bible. It was clear to the woman that her patient believed in God.

But now an inner voice prompted Nita: "Tell her."

She waited for the attendant to turn around.

"Do you know something? I'm going to get well," she mouthed carefully.

The attendant smiled with kindness and sorrow at once, as if to say, "I would like to believe it if I could."

"Yes," she answered, "that's why I've been working so hard, day and night, for so many months. What else do you think I'm doing this for?"

Nita was amused. "Do you know my God is going to heal me?" she asked.

The woman's face drooped pathetically as if to say, "What a shame, you hopeless vegetable, that you're losing your mind as well." But she recovered in a moment, shook her head solemnly, and said, "Yes."

Nita knew better. She had not taken her seriously at all. Nita decided to make a more lasting impression on her.

"Bring me a piece of paper and a pen."

Now the woman laughed. It was comical for Nita to make such a request, with her fingers twisted like pretzels. But she brought a pen and the cardboard backing of a scratch pad to humor her, and slipped the pen through the fingers as best she could, under her first and third fingers. Nita could not lift her hand off the bed, so the attendant slipped the paper between the bedsheet and Nita's hand. Then, while she held the paper steady, Nita summoned every ounce of available will power and painstakingly dragged her hand across the page, scrawling a message:

FRIDAY, FEBRUARY 11TH, 1977 3:30 P.M.

The woman looked at it quizzically.

"Keep it," Nita said without explanation. "And don't keep it here. Keep it in your own room." She didn't want the woman to think when the day came that it had been tampered with in any way. She wanted her to know, beyond any shadow of doubt, that Nita's God had done what He said He was going to do.

She wondered whether to tell Colton—wondered whether she would feel the necessary release from the Lord when he arrived later in the morning.

She heard him come through the front door, and she knew his routine. He always paused to quiz the attendant, to find out how many teaspoons of broth Nita had taken, how many times she had vomited or fainted or choked for air. Then he walked on into Nita's room, and she expected to hear the usual opening question: "How are you today?" But Colton had been talking to his Father, and He had heard something.

"What did God tell you?" he asked Nita pointedly.

Nita was taken aback. But she answered him cunningly with a question of her own.

"What about?"

Colton looked through her.

"What did God tell you?" he said again, with demand.

Nita had not even hinted to Colton or Suzanne about the voice, nor its message, nor the confirmation she had received in Colton's church. But somehow Colton had sensed the turning of the tide. She grinned at him. She knew she was about to see a spectacle of jubilation; it was Colton's way.

"God told me He is going to heal me on the eleventh of February at 3:30 in the afternoon."

But Colton did not exult as she expected. Instead, he

stood there, mesmerized, humbled and quiet, taking in the full import of what she was saying, realizing that God was already in the process of doing something so miraculous that he could not completely grasp it.

"What do you want me to do about it?" he finally asked softly.

Nita began to share the thoughts and inclinations that God had given her. She wanted people present for the miracle, to witness what God was going to do. She wanted no unbelief in the vicinity when her Savior came to her—only the company of true believers.

"No doubting Thomases while the Great Physician is at work," she said emphatically.

She wanted her mother close by. And medical experts who could document the authenticity of the healing.

But she made it clear, wagging an imaginary finger in Colton's face: he was not to tell anyone what was going to happen. She did not want anyone around to talk disbelievingly. No one was to know about the miracle in advance. God had sealed her lips. Much later she would realize why God had silenced her. He didn't want anyone talking her out of her miracle.

The preacher and the patient agreed together and prayed together, then Colton left. Nita lay awake after he had gone, unable to calm the fomenting excitement she was feeling.

As far as she was concerned, she was already healed. She had already begun to exist in the future, her mind and body as free as they had ever been. She was already living beyond February 11th. She rejoiced constantly, brimming with anticipation. She was convinced her miracle was en route. Later, those closest to her would recall the change in her personality even before the healing.

She laughed when she thought of this happening to her—of all people! Nita had always been the most skeptical Spirit-filled Christian she knew. She called herself "doubting Thomas's oldest daughter." She had never easily swallowed the miracle stories. The fantastic tales of God's unusual workings were fine for others—but now she was caught in the middle of one!

The agony was not in believing it, but in not being able to tell her precious mother or her grieving brother. She looked at them, worn with anguish, their faces creased with months of worry, and she begged her Father to let her ease their burden. But no release came. Nita had learned the hard way to obey the Lord, and she knew God wanted her to hold her peace.

But even this peculiar sadness couldn't squelch her emotions and she never looked back. She was continuously bursting with excitement, as if the miracle had actually occurred.

Colton's guest, Syvelle Phillips, was still in town. He was one of the greatest believers in supernatural healing that Colton knew. Syvelle's own mother had been miraculously healed when he was a teenager. Colton asked Nita if she would allow him to bring his guest to the apartment to pray for her. She agreed. It was an honor.

Syvelle sat and looked at her with pity in his eyes. Besides her own deformities, she had attached deformities as well. She was surrounded by sandbags and wearing her hulking metal calipers, which ran the full length of her legs and kept them from shrinking to different sizes as her hands already had.

Syvelle ministered to her with bravado, then prayed for her.

Colton smiled a broad smile.

"I believe God is going to heal Nita," he said to Syvelle as the prayer came to an end.

Syvelle nodded pleasantly and smiled in general agreement, just as so many others had nodded and smiled so many times over the months, each time Colton had spoken in the fullness of faith.

Nita looked at the visitor and a little green light blinked on inside her. She knew she should tell this American preacher about the miracle. She related her story matter of factly.

Syvelle continued his nodding, but he couldn't hold the smile. He looked toward Colton, to see if he had accepted the whole story. It was clear that he had.

"Have you been reading Betty Baxter's story?" Syvelle asked her. Betty Baxter, had been healed dramatically years before in the United States and had also declared the date of her healing in advance.

"Yes, I have her tapes," Nita responded.

That was enough for Syvelle. He felt Nita had probably made herself believe her own story after dwelling on somebody else's.

Outside the apartment, the American preacher quizzed Colton. How could he go along with this date-setting business? Syvelle could accept the fact of Nita's eventual healing—but the audible voice, the date and the hour, were a little extreme. It probably was the subtle suggestion of the Baxter tapes combined with so many months of despair. It just couldn't be!

Colton was adamant. He would not be shaken from his position. Nita had heard God's voice and she would be well again at 3:30 on February 11.

Syvelle gave up on Colton and attached himself to Suzanne, Colton's wife. He talked to her pointedly about facing reality. He was concerned for his friend's health. Colton had been working feverishly on the new church building, and Syvelle was afraid that he would be shattered if the miracle failed to occur.

But there was nothing to be done. Colton could not be persuaded otherwise.

Finally Syvelle made Suzanne a final last-ditch offer.

"If the miracle doesn't happen, and it's too much for Colton to take, call me," the preacher said with genuine compassion. "I'll come back here to Sri Lanka and take him home with me to the States for a while. The rest might do him good."

Syvelle headed back to America alone, deeply concerned about the future of his friend Colton. This Asian girl could be the death of his dearest friend.

Nita would bring one more person into the elite sacred circle.

Brother Andrew, immortalized as "God's Smuggler," had been scheduled to speak at Colton's church on the ninth and tenth of February. Hundreds of people who never normally attended would show up to hear the renowned man of God who had carried thousands of Bibles behind the Iron Curtain. Nita had never met him, but she wanted to hear him, so on the first evening of his visit Colton's boys carried her up to the balcony of the church and put her in her obscure corner to avoid the limelight.

Throughout the sermon Nita felt Andrew's beautiful piercing blue eyes on her, as if he were scanning her brain. It made her again self-conscious about her physical condition—and embarrassed. Afterwards Colton brought Andrew up to the balcony and introduced them to each other.

Nita knew in a moment that this man should also bear the sacred trust. Quietly, with Colton interpreting her noiseless words, Nita shared the great sacred secret with Brother Andrew.

He exploded in praise to God. Probably more than any

of them, Brother Andrew was accustomed to the miraculous. Among other things, he had seen God close the eyes of communist border guards as he smuggled Bibles and other illegal religious tracts behind the Iron Curtain. But the news about Nita turned his spiritual motor on, and he poured out thanks to God in a bubbly unknown language.

In the sacred circle of trust there were four believers and one skeptic.

17
Hail and Farewell

The next day was a hard one. The time had come for Ted to go back to England, and for all Nita's petitioning before the Throne of Grace, she still had no freedom to tell him about the miracle that she knew would occur in only twenty-four hours. He was broken. It killed him to leave her, and yet he knew it was pointless to stay.

"Man, I gotta get back," she overheard him wearily telling a cousin. "I have only one day before I have to be back on the job. I've got to get myself together."

Nita longed to make him stay, to say, "Hey, big brother, be here, stay home." Instead, she kept silent.

Inside, she ached for him to be there at the most fantastic moment of her life. The three other men she had been able to tell—Colton, Syvelle, Andrew—Nita would have gladly exchanged for the privilege of telling Ted. But the release never came.

She wanted to see him off to England, but he refused. He didn't want his sister to be a spectacle at the airport, and he knew that the trip, short as it was by normal standards, would exhaust her. He knew they would both break down, and he knew how dangerous that could be for Nita's failing heart.

Suzanne came by and took her to her mother's home, to bid him farewell. She did not get out of the car—the ritual would have taken too long—so Ted walked down to the gate and said his good-byes. He held her hand, the same crooked little hand that he had so desperately flexed on that first day in Sri Lanka. He bent down and kissed her again and again, grieved but trying to keep cool, biting back the tears. She knew by his face that he thought he was seeing her for the last time. Nita hated it. She loved him.

Now he was gone.

Mrs. Edwards drove Ted to the airport. Colton and his family would be going to church again, and they didn't want Nita to be alone in her apartment after the ordeal, so they insisted on taking her with them for Brother Andrew's second service.

It was late. The main floor was already packed. The balcony was full. People were standing in the stairways, in the rear of the sanctuary, in the foyer, anywhere there was a square foot of space. Nita was petrified. For every person in the swarming church, there were two gawking eyes.

It had already been an emotionally devastating day. She was at the edge, ready to break.

"If I can't get into the balcony," Nita pleaded with soundless lips, "I want to go home!"

Suzanne comforted her patiently. "It will be all right. I'll stay right with you. I won't leave you for a moment."

And she began pushing Nita's wheelchair to the only available place in the entire building: directly in front of the pulpit.

The service had already begun: Colton was at the pulpit, motioning to Suzanne to come on, come on, it's okay.

Nita felt her numb face growing hot with shame as the people turned and squirmed to stare, row by row, as she rolled down the aisle. It was the Roman Forum, the circus, with the spectators packing the galleries for a gander at the freak. An international delegation occupied the front row. The military adviser to the nation's president sat a few seats away. All the big shots had turned out for Brother Andrew...and here she sat, strapped like a bizarre rag doll to a metal chair, her head slumped down to one side on the end of a neck made of rubber, and—absurdly— wearing sunglasses because of the constant tearing and the sensitivity she had developed to direct light.

Who among the hundreds of people could help but stare at the misshapen little creature in front of the pulpit, her bony legs encased in metal braces, her fingers misjointed, as if she had been assembled by a demented toymaker?

Nita was decimated. Already today she had watched her brother walk away in despair, and now this debacle. She had been out from under the public microscope for so long...she had successfully avoided the limelight for so many weeks...and now she was front and center.

The service ended and bedlam descended on the helpless girl. The rabid attention of well-meaning masses had always embarrassed her, and now she was engulfed in it. A thousand people pressed in to pat her on the head and say, "God bless you, we're praying for you." Several of the foreigners wrote her name down to carry back the exotic prayer request. But Nita suspected they only came by out of morbid curiosity to look on her misshapen body. She was itching to tell them all to lay off with the sobbing and start rejoicing.

"Hey, brothers and sisters!" she wanted to shout.

"Tomorrow at this hour, by the grace of God, I'll be walking!"

But she could no more tell her secret to these nameless throngs than she could tell her precious, troubled brother. Or mother. Instead, she was reduced to smiling blandly for the onlookers, secretly resenting their intrusion on her privacy.

If only she could have held them off one more day.

But God's hand had arranged the bizarre exhibition! More people saw Nita's deformed body in that single evening than had seen her in all the months of her captivity. Tonight she was an obituary—tomorrow she would be Page One.

After the service, Colton led his family and Brother Andrew and Nita to a late dinner on the lawn of the Fountain Café. Michaele played with Nita, rubbing soup on her lips and goofing around. He thought he saw Dr. Pieris, the cynical Buddhist neurophysician, at another table on the lawn.

"He's staring at you," Michaele insisted.

But the lights were too dim for Nita to see him. Michaele impishly wheeled her past the man: he averted his eyes as they went by. Yes, it was Pieris.

How ironic, Nita thought, that he would be among the last to see her in this condition. *If only Ted could be here instead*, she thought grimly, still pining over her brother's sad departure.

Brother Andrew, on the other hand, was soaring, gobbling his dinner and laughing and talking about Nita's impending miracle as if he were receiving the healing himself. Suddenly he pushed away from the table and leaned over to Colton.

"Is it all right if I hug that girl?"

"Of course, go right ahead!"

Brother Andrew bounded toward her, squeezed her tight, and burst forth in tongues, praising God and weeping with joy. He was going to fly out of Sri Lanka tonight, only hours before the miracle, but he knew it would happen, and he was gleeful.

Nita watched Andrew clapping his hands and praising his Father, and she was tickled by the happy demonstration. She sensed that God had given her this beautiful little encounter to lift her spirits at the end of her final trying day. Even in the slightest things, she knew, her Heavenly Father was still caring for her.

"The joy of the Lord is my strength," she often recited from Nehemiah 8:10. On this last night of captivity, with its particular sadness, the Lord was strengthening her with this expression of divine joy.

Still, it felt good to know that this was the last time she would have to watch someone else express what she was feeling. She was thankful already that very soon she would be able to reach out and touch these dear people just as they had reached out and touched her...to show love as freely as she felt it...and as freely as she had received it.

Nita sighed softly and closed her eyes. She longed for the perfect, gentle face of tomorrow.

18
The Divine Touch

Nita had lived that week as one continuous day, hardly able to sleep for the excitement and anticipation. She began counting off the hours some four days before the event, urging the clock to hurry, hurry. She wanted time to speed away, so her Jesus could touch her.

She could see it already in her mind's eye. She could see the gnarled fingers and toes straightening. She could see her hands growing strong and healthy. She could see these miserable skinny legs filling out and straightening. She could see the bloated stomach shrinking to its normal size. She could hear her voice returning. She could see her vision coming back. She could see movement. She could see herself walking.

She could see herself whole.

It was no problem to see it all. It required no imagination, no mental talent. She was very sure.

Thursday night was a waste as far as sleep was concerned. The sun may as well have never set. Nita checked the clock every few minutes, and filled the time in between with prayer and praises to her Lord. But the night lingered on like an unwanted guest and would not go away. Finally she could wait no longer. As the hour hand of the clock crawled toward five, she buzzed her sleepy attendant and had her turn on Radio Sri Lanka. She also wanted her big wristwatch set precisely. She wanted to be ready for her appointment. She trusted that God had given her the promise in Sri Lanka time!

As she lay there, the tension of anticipation steadily mounted. Again and again she looked at the time and each hour she reminded herself of the promise.

At ten o'clock: "In five and a half hours, I'm coming off this bed."

At eleven o'clock: "In four and a half hours, I'm coming off this bed."

At noon: "In three and a half hours, I'm coming off this bed. Glory to God!"

Nita asked the attendant to place her slippers next to her bed. They had rarely been worn in the past year. The attendant laughed.

"Oh, you're fixing to take a walk, eh?" she asked as she put them in place.

Obviously she had forgotten the piece of paper hidden somewhere in her bedroom, and Nita kept quiet. She would see soon enough what her Jesus was going to do.

The woman gave Nita her morning sponge bath on schedule, but her patient requested the afternoon ritual to be a bit early—perhaps 12:30? She wanted to be sure she was ready in plenty of time for her appointment with the gracious Great Physician.

At 12:30 Nita watched the attendant's hands rubbing the sponge across her lifeless flesh as she had for so very many days. She could see movement through her weakened eyes, but she could not feel the sponge.

Just three more hours, she said to herself, *and I'm going to be totally healed*. The confidence was absolute. She knew she would feel again in three hours, totally restored by God. Even the simple sensation of a sponge bath would be wonderful.

But maybe, Nita thought, *since God's power is so great. . . maybe I'm already a little healed right now*. The attendant finished her work and reached under Nita's body with both arms to roll her over. It had always been like lifting a sack of potatoes before. Nita decided to jack her head up off the pillow, to see how healed she was.

The muscles were as dead as ever. She couldn't move the first inch. She tried each mental lever in succession, but all the connections were still unplugged: no voice, no vision, no muscular control—nothing.

Still, her faith was solid. The oldest daughter of Doubting Thomas was vanquished. The faithless, scoffing university student had died, and in her place was a new creature, full of faith. It didn't occur to this new Nita to think, *Hey, it might not happen; I might not be healed*. God had short-circuited her doubting apparatus. The old Nita would have analyzed and fretted over such a leap from cripple to conqueror. But the new Nita was not trying to help God do His work at all. She could still recall the calm, authoritative voice that had given her the promise: "Nita, I'm going to raise you up to carry the gospel to Asia. I'm going to heal you on Friday the eleventh of February."

How she would ever take the gospel to Asia she had no idea. But of her healing, of the date and the hour, she was utterly sure. God had given her the supernatural gift of faith. For the new Nita, the healing had already happened. All that remained was the gathering of the evidence!

In the past the afternoon sponging had always led to the

same thing: the attendant would dress her in clean bed-clothes. Today Nita stopped her.

"Bring me my slacks."

She had planned it all, days in advance. She knew just what she would be wearing when Jesus came in: a simple light green shirt, and the same pair of black-and-white checked slacks that she had been wearing as she bumped down the stairs of St. Bede's.

The attendant looked at her hesitantly, skeptically. Nita had not worn slacks at all in nearly a year. She would have to remove the heavy metal calipers from her legs.

"Go ahead!" Nita said decisively. "And take those rotten sandbags as well."

After months of gross weight loss, the slacks hung on her like shower curtains. But Nita was content. To walk again wearing these same slacks would satisfy her sense of dramatic irony.

When the attendant had carefully lain her back down on the bed, fully dressed, her eyes immediately locked in again, magnet-like, on her wristwatch. Gradually, prayerfully, Nita's eyes closed for longer stretches, as she began to be enveloped in the awesome presence of God.

She was beautifully calm, resting on a cloud of assurance, lost in the love of her Heavenly Father. Again she was floating out into the beautiful Indian Ocean, resting happily on her daddy's shoulders, confident of his strength, sure of his love. There were no doubts to disturb the moment, no questions to interrupt the tranquility. The Father was there. Her Father was in firm and loving control.

As Nita slipped ever nearer to the heart of God, the chosen few who would witness the miracle began to assemble reverently around her.

At two o'clock, Colton and Suzanne arrived, solemn

and quiet. They knew this would soon be holy ground. It was clear from the glow of Nita's face that the transformation would soon begin. They didn't talk to her at all, but sat down and began to pray quietly.

Colton's secretary Beryl had interceded in prayer for Nita with unmatched fervor during her illness. Colton felt she should be present. She arrived and joined the graceful travail.

Two women doctors, stepped into the room. They were medical professionals who loved the Lord and who had examined and treated Nita during parts of her long ordeal. They had no hint of what was going to happen here; Colton had only invited them to a special time of prayer. They were honored. They knew Nita Edwards was in seclusion and only a select few had ever been behind these doors.

Colton's youngest son Michaele arrived without his brother. He sat outside Nita's bedroom door to make room for the others. After a while he got thirsty and, with no idea of what he would miss, left to get a milkshake.

At three o'clock, Colton read a passage of Scripture. Even today, no one who was in the room remembers what passage he read. The presence of God was already so overwhelming that everything else was thoroughly submerged.

Then Colton knelt beside the bed to pray, and the others followed his lead—except for Dr. Sudo, who because of her pregnancy sat in a chair.

Nita's mother knelt to her daughter's left, closest to her. Colton and Suzanne were on the right, toward the foot of the bed. Days before, Nita had teased them about keeping their distance. "You never know what the Lord's going to do." It would turn out to be wise advice.

The room was filled with prayer and a sense of awe, and

the supernatural transformation began. At 3:20 Nita looked at her watch for the last time. She knew beyond any shred of doubt that her days as a paralytic cripple were fast coming to an end. In that moment, by faith, she crossed the chasm between earth's time and God's time. And she was suddenly living in a capsule of eternity. Minutes and seconds became meaningless as the Holy Spirit bathed her in supernatural life, making her more alive than she had ever been.

Nita felt her spirit being lifted, and she soared with it. Her paralyzed throat was gurgling and rasping praises to God. She was unable to stop bursting with praise.

Colton opened his eyes, amazed to hear it. In all his months of fiery ministry to her, and remembering all the people who had stood by her bed prophesying and speaking in tongues, he had never seen Nita open up in her worship. She had never even led in prayer. She had wept, she had entered into prayer, but her Episcopalian propriety had always prevailed...she had always been careful not to engage in that "raucous behavior."

Until now. Even without a voice, she was crying out, before the Throne, without regard to the people around her...in keen anticipation of what God was about to do for her.

The power of God invaded the room, from the right side of her bed, like a ball of fire. The glory of God burst in, flooding that tiny space with such intensity that the inhabitants were swept up in it, and overcome by it. It was like looking directly at the noonday sun, and only being able to take in a tiny fraction of the radiance.

The air was charged with a fantastic burst of electricity. Nita's bed began to vibrate with the energy of God's presence, and she felt a million volts of power coursing through her body. Every cell, every fiber, every tissue of her body pulsed with it. Wave after wave rolled through the full length of her. She was oblivious to her surroundings, to the others. She was longing to see Jesus.

Just at 3:30, He came into the room with blinding glory, phenomenal brilliance, impossible radiance. Nita gazed into His face, and everything within her struggled to reach out to Him, to draw even one bit closer to Him. Her healing was no more a factor. She was unaware of her own physical condition. Her physical realm had evaporated. She only longed to touch Him...to connect somehow with that fabulous source of light and love.

In later years, when Nita tried to talk about it, she was never able to satisfy herself with words. Nothing ever came close to capturing the majesty of those moments. But as she struggled to describe the encounter, her arms often ached with the tension of that beautiful longing.

As she looked at Him, He moved toward her. She was suspended in time and space, filled beyond capacity by the unfathomable love of God. He came to the foot of her bed, and then He reached out with a nail-scarred hand.

And He touched her.

One time.

19
Celebration

The chains of paralysis exploded away as Nita rocketed out over the end of her bed.

She landed on her knees with a thud, and her first sensation was the cold, hard tile floor beneath her. The divine warmth of the touch of her Lord had suddenly given way to this startling awakening. In the days to come she would realize that God had touched her so warmly only to thrust her into a ministry of fervent intercessory prayer in the cold real world.

Her knees had not been bent in over a year; now they were bent before her Jesus. Her hands, useless for so long, were now straightened, upraised, worshiping God. Her voice had been still; now her mouth began to fill with heavenly words, tumbling out in a bubbly fountain of praise. For the first time in her life, she was leading others in prayer.

Mrs. Edwards had felt the bed vibrating and opened her eyes. There before her, she saw Nita's withered left hand, the tiny one, spring to life. The mother watched, awe-struck, as her crippled little girl grasped the bed covers and threw them off—then catapulted out of bed.

The doctor who was kneeling heard the rustling of linens and looked up to see Nita leaping past her.

Beryl had looked up at the same moment, and as Nita went by the secretary's eyes fell on Nita's oversized wristwatch. It was precisely 3:30.

The Great Physician was on time for His appointment.

Suzanne heard the action and opened her eyes. Nita was not in the bed. She glanced immediately to the foot of the bed, and saw her dropping to her knees with the momentum of her leap.

Dr. Sudo, sitting against the wall, heard Nita praying—something she had never heard her do. She looked at the bed and found it empty. There was Nita, kneeling at the foot of it, worshiping her Healer in glowing ecstacy.

The Buddhist nurse was in the habit of checking in on Nita every few minutes, regardless of who was visiting. She had peeked in twice since three o'clock, and each time found the prayer meeting in progress, with Nita looking comfortable in her bed.

When she stepped in again, she stopped in the doorway—furious. These lunatic Christians had lugged the poor cripple out and propped her up against the foot of her bed to pray!

Young Michaele came back to find Nita on her knees, and immediately he knew what had happened. He smacked his forehead, chagrined. She had asked him to be there, and he had blown it.

Nita was not conscious of the others praying and worshiping God. She had tuned out this earthly realm a full ten minutes before, and was engulfed by the presence and the power of her Lord, the Almighty God.

Shortly after four, Colton suddenly jumped up.

"We've prayed long enough!" he declared smiling, his face wet with tears. "Now it's time to celebrate!"

Everyone stood—and Nita stood.

The room fell silent for a moment as the people absorbed the shock of what they were seeing. Now that Nita was healed, the rest of them were paralyzed. Like Peter on the Mount of Transfiguration, they could not quite yet take in the miracle.

Mrs. Edwards blanched as Nita took her first step. Suzanne—even knowing what to expect—instinctively reached out to help her. Nita drew away. She felt the strength of ten tigers. She was ready to go jogging, to climb up the roof. She was fully empowered and ready to roar.

But her guests were still stunned. Nita stepped toward them, kissing each one in turn and mumbling the only verse of Scripture that came to her mind, "He is faithful that promised," the obscure little portion of Hebrews 10:23 that the King James Version relegates to parentheses.

"He is faithful that promised."

Nita's mother was dazed. She had never expected this.

"Mama," Nita whispered as she embraced her tearfully, "He is faithful that promised."

The Buddhist attendant was standing in the doorway, clutching the door frame as if she were about to faint. She was crying in quiet hysteria, unable to believe that she had just seen Nita stand up. She cried for forty minutes—immoveable. Nita slipped her arms around the woman she had never been able to touch, and then, ignoring the Buddhist standards of propriety, kissed her lightly on the cheek.

"Didn't I tell you my Jesus was going to heal me?"

The woman jumped. She had forgotten. She broke loose, pivoted, and charged back to her room.

Michaele took the opportunity to grab his dear friend and check out the Physician's work. Nita sat on the bed and let Michaele administer her first physical exam—putting each limb through its paces, giving her an impromptu vision test. Satisfied, the teenager began boxing with her merrily. Nita laughed with him. When they started arm-wrestling, though, Suzanne intervened.

"Michaele, stop that!"

"What do you mean?" he asked, genuinely surprised. "God healed her! She can take it!"

And with childlike faith, he went back to boxing with her.

The match was cut short as the Buddhist attendant came to the door. She held the scrap of cardboard in her hands.

"What is written here?" she asked one of the doctors, still unable to fathom the miracle.

The doctor read the scrawled message aloud:

FRIDAY, FEBRUARY 11TH, 1977 3:30 P.M.

The attendant began weeping profusely, her eyes racing frantically.

"She told me!" the woman cried. "She told me! She told me several days ago! And today she made me get her slippers out! Now I know why!"

She ran out of the apartment, compelled to talk about what she had just seen. Up and down the street, from door to door, the electrified Buddhist woman declared the miracle—to neighbors, to passersby, to anyone who would listen—perhaps the first Buddhist evangelist.

Nita's mother was the next to leave the celebration. She hurried home to begin making phone calls and sending cables—contacting every person she had ever asked to pray, and announcing that the answer had come! First she would call Ted—if he had even arrived in London yet. And then there were Sonny, and Auntie Vivian, and Uncle Jay and Auntie Patty in Nigeria....

Colton's older son Eran drove up, and as soon as Nita heard the car, her mental wheels began turning. To play a joke on him, she hid behind the door as he walked in. When she stepped into view, Eran shouted with fright. He thought she had finally died, and he was seeing her ghost. Everyone exploded in laughter.

Eventually the super-charged meeting broke up, as Colton's family and Beryl and the two doctors made their way home.

When Nita was left alone in the apartment, she began to walk . . . into the kitchen, around to the bathroom, into the foyer, back to the bedroom. Such a novelty—to walk! Her waist, terribly thin from months of weight loss, would not hold up her slacks. Even as she clutched them with one hand they sagged around her hips and hung about three inches too long. But she rolled them up and continued her happy pacing for hours. Like a newly hooked jogger, she must have covered ten miles that night within her small apartment.

As she went she filled the place with praise and thanksgiving, dwelling on the incredible goodness of her Lord. At times during the marathon walk, she stopped to sit down and examine her fingers or her toes in amazement. She pinched herself. She scratched. She touched household objects just for the thrill of feeling them. The sense of touch was like a new toy and Nita, the child, was inclined to wear its batteries all the way down on the first night!

Mrs. Edwards, having exhausted all the people she could possibly call or cable, hurried to her kitchen to fix up something special for her daughter. Soon she reappeared at Nita's door to drop off some food. Nita was touched by the sentiment as she opened the container—it was shrimp! With a flourish, she actually fed them to herself. It was a far cry from the last time she had eaten shrimp, when her mother had to put them in her mouth for her in the hospital.

And she wanted to indulge in one more temporal delight. Nita headed for the bathroom, locked herself in, and drew a hot bath. She played in the water with complete abandon, flapping at the soap suds and splashing like a happy baby, reveling in her newly-sensitive skin. They were luxurious moments, except for her nervous attendant pounding on the door every few minutes to make sure she was still healed and okay.

After lounging lazily in a hot tub, Nita went back to her bedroom and sat down in the visitor's chair. She had never sat in it before. It sure beat the wheelchair! She picked up her Bible and opened it. For the first time in a long time, she could see clearly the words of Psalm 23, the words that had buoyed her spirit from the beginning: "Yea, though I walk through the valley of the shadow of death, I will fear no evil: for thou art with me."

She thumbed over to Isaiah 40. Here, too, she had found solace many times when the waiting seemed futile. But now, she had the promise in hand: "He giveth power to the faint; and to them that have no might he increaseth strength. . . .

"But they that wait upon the Lord shall renew their strength; they shall mount up with wings as eagles; they shall run, and not be weary; and they shall walk, and not faint."

For so long, it had only been an elusive, haunting

promise. . . now she was living on the fact side of faith.

Nita sat worshipfully before the Lord for a long time before preparing for bed. It was thrilling to be able to do this for herself after being exposed and reexposed so many times. It was glorious to brush her own teeth, to plump her own pillow, and finally—after craving privacy for so long—to shut her door.

She sank into the coziness of her bedsheets. Tonight, for the first time ever, this huge bed was a friendly place.

Later on, when people asked her if she was afraid to get back into that bed—afraid that she might wake up a cripple again the next morning—the question invariably surprised her. Her body was so full of energy that night, so vibrant with God's supernatural power, that the idea of a relapse never entered her mind. Instead she lay there, enveloped in the afterglow of the presence of her Lord.

She sang to Him softly in the darkness until she fell asleep. The song had been one of her favorites from her early days in the hospital:

> How can I say thanks for the things you have done for me?
> Things so undeserved, yet you give to prove your love for me.
> The voices of a million angels could not express my gratitude;
> All that I am and ever hope to be, I owe it all to thee.
>
> To God be the glory; To God be the glory,
> To God be the glory For the things He has done.
> With His blood He has saved me,
> With His power he has raised me,
> To God be the glory For the things He has done.

Just let me live my life,
Let it be pleasing Lord, to Thee;
And should I gain any praise,
Let it go to Calvary.

With His blood He has saved me,
With His power He has raised me,
To God be the glory For the things He has done!

Buddist Lady Ascilin Nona - Medical attendant (few days after healing).

20
Reminders

It is a medical fact that anyone who suffers paralysis in the legs for three months or more suffers muscular atrophy and must undergo physical therapy to regain his normal gait.

Nita Edwards was scientifically documented as completely paralyzed for over a year. Her normal gait returned on Friday, February 11, 1977, at 3:30 p.m., Sri Lanka time, the very moment of her healing.

She bore three reminders of her personal holocaust. First, she had lost weight, and had to have new clothes tailored, but eventually she gained back the lost pounds.

Second, the soles of her feet were tender after more than a year of non-use. For a few weeks after her healing, it tickled her to walk. But this reminder disappeared as well.

The third reminder is still with her. To this day, she bears scars on her body from the pricking, cutting, and "testing" of the medical experts.

Nita Edwards told her story in public for the first time in church the day after the miracle. She was bashful about appearing in public, but she felt God had given her something too astounding to conceal.

Many who had scoffed at the constant prayer requests for Nita were in the congregation that day. The youth of the church experienced powerful revival as a result of her testimony.

Nita's Buddhist attendant had no choice but to accept Jesus Christ as her personal Savior. She is an active, enthusiastic Christian today.

Brother Andrew jumped for joy when word reached him that Nita Edwards had been healed. He never doubted.

Back in the United States, when Nita and Syvelle Phillips met in person for the first time since the miracle, Syvelle sobbed openly. He was thrilled that he had been wrong.

Sandy Koelmeyer rejoiced and wept when Nita called her with the news. Father Shirley beamed with joy when he first encountered his old friend made new.

The day of Nita's healing, the first call her mother made was to England. Ted had arrived home only ninety minutes before, still emotionally strung out, when the phone rang.

"Son, Sissy got healed," she said breathlessly. "She can walk."

His response was instantaneous. "Are her hands normal?"

Nita's crooked fingers had made the deepest impact on him.

He was hurt, however, when he found out that Nita had known of the impending miracle and failed to tell him about it or to keep him in Sri Lanka for it. As her brother, he saw no reason to have been deprived of that. There was a strain in the relationship between brother and sister for a long time afterwards. But overpowering family love and Ted's respect for the power of God eventually mended the tested relationship.

Dr. Shan, the specialist who had scarred Nita's body, soon heard about the miracle. Each time Nita visited people in the hospital later, Dr. Shan studiously avoided her.

Dr. Pieres, the Buddhist neurophysician, told the medical staff that her healing was a hoax, a physchological stunt. He crossed Nita's path a few times in public places in the ensuing years, but he pretended not to know her, and when she confronted him directly, refused to speak to her at all. To do otherwise, presumably, would mean admitting that his therapy had failed—and that indeed Nita's recovery was a miracle.

But the facts were undeniable, and the two doctors who witnessed the miracle arranged to have the case fully documented. In the end, there was only one truth that could be absolutely verified: Nita Edwards was no longer a hostage in her own body.

She was free!

She is free!

PART III

And ye shall know that I am in the midst of Israel,
and that I am the Lord your God, and none else:
and my people shall never be ashamed.
Joel 2:27

First anniversary Feb. 11, 1978 Thanksgiving service.

Crusade follow-up in Church by Public demand

One week after her healing, in the same room.

Afterword

Magnificent Obsession

Ron Hembree

The four of us huddled around the small table in the busy Orlando, Florida, coffee shop. We were bone tired, but bouyant because the "Nita book" was about wrapped up. We had carefully chased the story across two continents and now all that was left to do was the epilogue. But, it was a troublesome task because it is not easy to close the "Book of Acts." Luke had the same problem.

Mark, Nita, Doug Brendel and I had wrestled with the difficulty until the wee hours of the morning before giving up in exhaustion. We had followed Mark around the country with his heavy speaking schedule so we could snatch the hours needed to complete the story. Our odyssey had taken us to Toronto, Chicago, back to Toronto, to Charlotte, Atlanta, and now Orlando, Florida. We were not only exhausted from the strain of writing but also traveling. But it was more than exhaustion. The epilogue simply would not come together.

Much of the problem came in trying to sort out what

should be included. We still had so much more to tell. There was that strange and secret visit of a mysterious messenger from God that haunted us! Should we share that? We decided not to because it was still too early to properly evaluate her impact. . . a later book would have to bear that remarkable story. And there were the still unanswered questions of just how Nita would fit into the coming great Third World revival.

We could only speculate on this, and our human imagination would only tarnish the glow of what God no doubt will do. There could be no room in our book for guesses no matter how carefully thought out.

Should we tackle the thorny problem of the criticism against Nita's decision to come to America? There were those in Asia who could not understand why she would come to finish her education when time was so short and the Asian need so great. Perhaps we should deal with this problem—but how? Would our epilogue satisfy those critics, or would it merely seem like a defence for her decision?

Then, there was that strange spiritual kinship that God developed between Mark and Nita. All through the book project Mark would call me or cable from India, saying, "POURING MY HEART OUT FOR YOU IN PRAYER FOR THE BOOK, LOVE MARK." He talked about her all the time and begged prayers for her.

For all of our training and experience, we still could not get a handle on how to end the book.

Our waitress patiently brought another round of coffee even though we had long overstayed the allotted breakfast hour. I'm sure she wished we would leave to free the table for tippers who would exceed her expectations from we four. We sipped slowly and verbally battered around different ideas.

Our tedium must have created some tension, for at that moment, just a brief apostrophe of time, something happened that would burn into my spirit and let me know what the Nita book was really all about.

Mark had started to speak when his raspy voice broke down into a whisper. I looked up and saw scalding tears roll down his ragged cheeks and splash on the table. His whole face seemed to collapse in a chasm of agony. I tensed with concern, but I knew Mark well enough to sense he was opening his deepest soul and letting us take a small look inside the sacred secrets of his life. It was as if some divine sword, for some unknown reason, clave open his bleeding heart and the pain of that incision forced tears, choked his voice, and distorted his cherubic features.

We leaned close physically to his broken whisper. But more, our souls strove to sense what was stirring Mark so deeply.

"Please forgive me, dear ones," Mark whispered. "I am embarrassed, I didn't want to cry. I must tell you why I'm so tied to Nita's miracle."

He stopped to try to gain his composure. Unable to do so he plunged ahead.

"I'm so afraid, I'm so afraid of forgetting the spiritual. For so long now I've been spending so many hours in the natural—building the hospital, feeding the starving. I don't want to forget the most important of all."

A heart-shattering sob exploded from his pent up soul. He couldn't go on. Mark's whole frame began to react to his heartbreak. Suddenly he jumped up and rushed from the room. He had not wanted to embarrass us with his shattered emotions in a public restaurant.

I knew Mark would be back. But, I also knew something else. I knew he had not slept after our late night session. At about 2:30 we had given up and gone to bed. But Mark had gone on praying, searching, asking. His soul was so wrapped up in this story, sleep was impossible. It bound him as a prisoner and haunted him every step of his day. Slowly it began to dawn on me why Nita's story meant so much to *him*.

We waited, not daring to speak a word. Nita's head was bowed and tears streaked her beautiful brown face. Doug sat solemnly staring down at the floor not knowing how to handle the deep emotion of the moment. I was stunned because I had not been able to see it before. We sat silent and waited to let the significance of what had so suddenly happened sink in. Mark's great heart was broken in two. My mind whirled with what had so deeply touched my great friend.

Mark had become a legend in humanitarian circles. His sudden acclaim had burst on the western world only rather recently. For over twenty-five years he had labored in the world's worst slum, Calcutta, virtually unrecognized. But all that was different now. Two best-sellers had been written about his work and himself. A movie was made of his accomplishments and television crews commissioned from the western world had wheeled through the bustees to catch a glimpse of the great missionary—humanitarian.

"Readers' Digest" contracted a writer to do a major book section story of "The Apostle of Calcutta." The administrators were so impressed with his work they sent their Ottawa, Canada, editor to Calcutta to verify all that was written. After days of being with Mark, the editor asked, "What is it Mark that I feel coming out of you? It is like electricity! Like some kind of life."

The editor had ample reasons to be impressed. There is that great Christian hospital Mark built in the "City of the Dreadful Night." It has been so successful and of such high quality nearly all of India knows of it and seeks admission there when ill. The nation's leaders prefer his hospital over all others.

There is the feeding program where each morning Mark feeds twelve thousand starving children. Many of them would die without this man. Mark had seen the starving, hollow-eyed children and he could not leave them to die. While others talked of doing something, Mark marched on the horrible holocaust of human suffering—giving milk and a meal. Twelve thousand more human beings live every day because of this man.

When Doug Wead researched his best-seller about Mark on the streets of Calcutta an old Hindu stopped him.

"Young man," the toothless man said, wagging a bony finger in the writer's face, "You people think Jesus lives in North America. But you're wrong."

The old man went on: "Jesus lives in India. You come with me tomorrow and watch as Pastor Buntain dips the milk and gives the food, and you'll see Jesus too."

There is the school of six thousand youngsters Mark has started in a country where over 60 percent of the population can neither read nor write.

There are the industries Mark began, and sustains, to employ seven hundred and eighty Indians. He provides work for these—his people—in a city where men and women work feverishly from sun up to sun down for a single bowl of rice.

There are the forty village churches, schools, and medical centers surrounding Calcutta that Mark has started and keeps going.

We could go on, and talk of the home for troubled youth he has established...or the mobile hospitals he sponsors and sends weekly to the bustees of Calcutta. There is the literature program touching the whole teeming country of India.

There is the two-and-one-half-million dollar budget he

raises annually in North America and pours into the broken city of Calcutta. None of this money finds its way into Mark's own pocket. He lives in the same apartment he lived in when he went to Calcutta over twenty-six years ago. It is three stories up, by stairs only, and much of the time is without water. When in America Mark buys his clothes at K-Mart and wears seven-dollar slacks and three-dollar shirts. People give him clothing but he continually gives it away to those who are needy.

Mark has lifted lepers, healed the sick through his medical facilities, and raised those who were dead to some hope of a future. He haunts the bustees and stalks the streets to haul out the helpless and hopeless and he gives them life. Like his female counterpart in Calcutta, Mother Teresa, he is a living legend to the people there.

It is for all of this and more that Mark is highly acclaimed, publicly praised, and nominated for his country's highest honor, "The Order of Canada." Millionaires now vie for the chance to dine with him. Senators and congressmen rearrange their schedules to talk with him. Movie stars ask him to their homes. He has the world at his feet.

But Mark's world is Calcutta.

Several pregnant and silent minutes passed as I pondered those thoughts. Our waitress, not knowing the dynamics, but sensing something strange and wonderful, poured more coffee, darting her glance from face to face. She sought the secret in one of the lingering trio. . . not finding it she shrugged and left.

Mark returned, but he was still shaken. He sat down carefully saying, "I'm sorry, dear ones. Please forgive me." He worked his fingers in that familiar kneading action so well known to those who love him. Mark prayed. But, he always prays.

He started again, trying to carefully control his voice, telling us why Nita and her miracle were so special to him. Nita was sent to Mark when the applause of the world began to fill his ears. He had seen what popularity had done to others and realized that more prophets have been silenced by prosperity and popularity than persecution. He had been deeply searching his heart to always be sure he would never sacrifice the spiritual for the natural. Then Nita came.

Mark's heart is consumed by a burning love for the lost souls of Calcutta and all of Asia—and in Nita's miracle he sees the bombshell that will detonate a great explosion of spiritual revival throughout that whole continent. Her miracle is an ever-startling reminder to him that the spiritual is all that really matters.

In Asia, that repository of many gods, people listen lightly and easily accept another god. Jesus just becomes an addition to the collection, like Kali or Krishna. Mark knows that there must not be merely an acceptance of Jesus, but a turning away from all other gods to serve Him alone. The only way the Asian mind can clearly comprehend this necessity is for them to see the dramatic power of Christ that supersedes any other god or power known to them. This is why Nita's remarkable miracle means so much to Mark. Here is a dramatic miracle that clearly calls Asians to the awareness of who Jesus is. He is not *another* god, He is the King of Kings and Lord of Lords.

Mark Buntain will never give up his humanitarian ventures. They are as much a part of him as his own heart and hands. He will always feed the hungry, heal the sick and lift the load of physical suffering. These are overflows of compassion from a heart crammed full of love and concern. He could no more turn from the needy than make the day turn from the light.

"I must give myself more to evangelism," Mark pleaded, not to us, but to his heavenly Father. I began to realize that day that Mark will never comfortably fit into the role of the "great humanitarian" so many of us try to press him into. This is because his life's passion is to preach the cross and the Christ he so passionately loves. Now, God has sent him Nita, and her presence is a constant reminder to Mark of the great Third World revival he has prayed for now for over a quarter of a century.

Our marathon breakfast finally broke up. Nita went to her room and Mark to his. Doug and I talked. We knew that when Mark finally stands before the Lord he loves, it will be a strange account of his life that Mark will give. On that day Mark will not tell the Lord about the hospital he built or the children he fed. He will not speak of the great school he started or the lepers he lifted and helped to heal. Rather, Mark will simply bow before his Lord and whisper through his tears, "Thank you, Jesus, for letting me go to Calcutta and to Asia to tell others about your love."

We still do not have the end of our book. But, I guess that is okay. Luke could never finish "The Acts" because the acts of the Holy Spirit are still going on. That's where we are. We will hear from Nita again. I don't know when or how, but she will be part of the coming great Third World revival. We will hear of Colton too—and others in this book. We will hear!

Then, there is Mark. Mark will continue to weep and work his life out for the Lord. He will continue to be criticized and canonized. But, I believe Mark too is a vital key to revival in all of Asia. He was the third face in

Colton's vision. But, for me, there is an even more personal reason for holding this conviction.

In the final days of building this book our writing team was in Charlotte. We stayed in a lovely chalet loaned to us for the day by the PTL Club. We had worked long into the night on the book, and finally, we broke up to go to bed. Nita went to her room, and we to ours. The house was dark and silent except for one haunting sound.

My room was directly above Mark's. As usual he was praying. But, this time there were no words to his prayers. I could only hear groans of agony from his soul for lost Asia. I was strangely moved by those soul sounds of intercession for the lost souls half a world away. The brown, seeking, hungry, haunted faces of Asia paraded before me.

I saw the blind and groping beggar lift his empty cup mouthing a cry for a simple bowl of milk.

I saw the zombie-teenage girl shuffle by me, unseeing, on her way to death, unaware of the vomit and excrement blotching her ragged dress.

I saw the tired and hunger-worn mother offer her milkless breast to the crying, hollow-eyed infant she held.

I saw the children, who did not even know their own names, dig through the garbage of Calcutta for a scrap of something to eat.

I saw the haunted and harried Guru searching, seeking for some unknown elusive light.

I also saw the other face of India, sophisticated, subtle, sumptuous; sick of the death around it, but honestly not knowing how to heal the hurts.

I saw Asia, dear Asia, as Mark calls it, in its sickness and sorrow, waiting for some touch to cure it from its interminable paralysis of suffering.

But in the spirit I saw something else. I don't know how

it will be done, but I saw the prayer of my dear friend, Mark, being answered. Asia will know revival soon. The suffering and sadness of that mass of humanity will be touched by our Master's nail-scarred hand because He cares. He cares.

I slipped into a warm and welcomed sleep still listening to plaintive cries coming from the room below me.

Mark was weeping again.

Ron Hembree is author of Mark, the biography of Dr. Mark Buntain.

PART IV

For we have not followed cunningly
devised fables, when we made known
unto you the power and coming
of our Lord Jesus Christ, but
were eyewitnesses of
His majesty.
II Peter 1:16

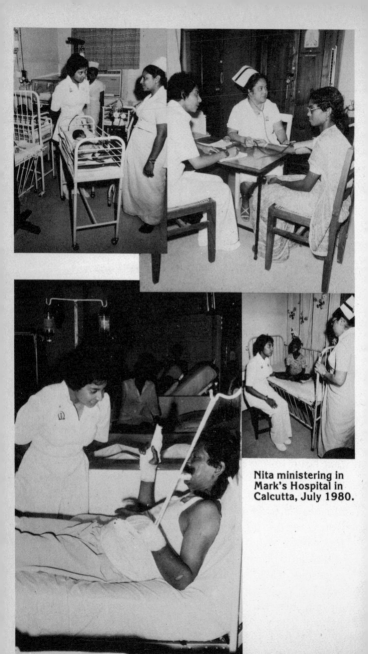

Nita ministering in Mark's Hospital in Calcutta, July 1980.

Faith on the Line

Brother Andrew

I believe in miracles. That is as much a general statement as saying, "I believe the Bible," or "I believe the Bible from cover to cover." Then suddenly you are faced with a crisis situation, and your whole faith seems to be on trial. You stand there helplessly, groping around and calling for help, and then at that moment, where is your faith? In God, in His Word, in miracles?

That evening, I had a meeting in Pastor Colton's great church in Colombo. Somewhere to my right I could see that beautiful girl in a wheelchair, but what did I know about what God had told her? The story has been unfolded in this book. At that moment I did not know, but after my preaching on the Great Commission, Pastor Colton came to me and asked me to please pray with Nita for tomorrow God was going to heal her.

Basically, it is always a tremendous privilege and challenge and an act of confidence when anybody asks you to pray for a sick person—in fact, to pray for anything or anyone. But there she was; a lovely young girl, almost completely paralysed, telling me that the next day she was going to be healed, that God had spoken to her, that she knew the will of God; and asking me to pray for her.

There you stand. Is it going to depend on my prayer, on my faith, or her faith? Can I be a hindrance if I do not have faith, if I do not pray? Shall I pray without faith? Or shall I simply obey—pray, commit myself to God and this person for whom I pray? Call on the Name of Jesus Christ who can do anything, any time, to anyone?

I did not doubt. But to say that I believed was another thing. However, I obeyed because God told me to. So that evening I prayed with Nita, bending over her wheelchair and laying hands on her.

The next day, the plane had taken me back to my native Holland. But a great friend of mine, Francis Grim, the founder and president of the International Hospital Christian Fellowship, happened to be in a meeting the following evening in Pastor Colton's church. He is a man of God who believes in the Healer and in healing, by miracles and by the medical profession, but not himself exactly a man who prays often with the sick for divine healing. But, to his utter amazement, he saw that evening a totally different Nita—not in a wheelchair any more, not in braces, not paralysed, but walking, speaking, testifying, and electrifying that audience by the word of her testimony. God had kept His word, not because I believe in miracles, not because my faith was shaken, but because God is God: He speaks and His Word is creative; He touches and there is healing; He comes and there is new life. And then He calls into His service.

Nita, that's what He has done for you! He has called you to Himself for His service. You've traveled more than you ever imagined you would do. God has used you, and He will use you even more. Those great lands in the

East—India, Sri Lanka and other Asian nations—are going to produce men and women of God, of whom you are one. So let's just keep looking to the Lord to do greater miracles, in our lives and through our ministries.

Dear reader, I pray you have opened your heart as you read this book. God is the same in Jesus Christ, yesterday, today and forever—in Asia, Europe, America, China, Africa, Israel or wherever you live.

Faith on Fire

H. Syvelle Phillips

The Book of Acts has no formal conclusion. Many believe the reason is that God wanted to convey the idea that the miraculous ministry of the Holy Spirit, which is so evident in the book of Acts, would go on century after century without interruption or conclusion.

Jesus Christ is indeed the same yesterday, today, and forever. The days of miracles and divine visitation did not cease with the death of the New Testament era apostles. While the Canon of Scriptures closed the record, the Acts of the Holy Spirit is still being written today.

The true story of the miraculous healing of Nita Edwards is strong evidence of the glorious fact that God is answering prayer and honoring faith today.

I had the privilege of visiting Nita Edwards in her home in Columbo, Sri Lanka, on two occasions approximately three weeks before she was healed. Nita was wasted away under the scourge of her affliction. When I saw her, she weighed only 76 lbs. and could only move one hand and her head just a bit.

In spite of the devastating ordeal Nita went through, she had a beautiful smile and trust in God. After prayer, Nita told me the date and the hour she would be healed, February 11, 1977 at 3:30. I must confess that my faith for such a miracle was not as strong as the bold faith of Nita Edwards that filled the room that day.

Shortly after my return to America I received a letter from Rev. Colton Wickramaratne that said, "Dear Pastor Syvelle Phillips, just as I said, on February 11, Nita was healed by the mighty power of God."

This healing was so instantaneous and complete, it can be said that Nita Edwards' body was recreated and restored to the same healthy and vivacious state as before the accident.

Every time I see this charming young lady who has a radiant smile, a spiritual glow and good health, I say, "Thank God the Book of Acts has no formal conclusion."

Jesus Christ lives and the Holy Spirit is ministering to human needs in love and power.

Syvelle Phillips is founder of "Evangel Bible Translation" and an internationally known leader in the charismatic movement.